MONTESSORI
AND THE SPECIAL CHILD

R. C. OREM

Montessori and the Special Child

CAPRICORN BOOKS

New York

DEDICATION

Instead of giving out what she has in herself, the teacher must bring out the full possibilities of the children.

Maria Montessori, *The Advanced Montessori Method*. Vol. 2, New York, Stokes, 1917, p. 44.

This book is affectionately dedicated to Lena L. Gitter—Montessori mother (and grandmother) . . . lecturer, teacher trainer, researcher, author, and translator.

For forty years, Lena has conveyed the Montessori message in word and deed—from Vienna to the Virgin Islands; from London to Louisiana—to parents, professionals, and pupils.

Truly a dedicated directress, and one of the greatest living examples of the "new teacher," she has observed the child and discovered an emergent man.

A Prediction by R. Buckminster Fuller

There will come the time when the proper education of children, by a glorified system of spontaneous education of choice, similar to the Montessori System, will be made possible. Children, as well as grown-ups, in their individual, glorified, drudgery-proof homes in Labrador, the Tropics, the Orient or where you will, to which they can pass with pleasure and expedition by means of ever-improving transportation, will be able to tune in their television and radio to the moving picture lecture of, let us say, President Lowell of Harvard; the professor of mathematics of Oxford; or the doctor of Indian antiquities at Delhi, etc. Education by choice, with its marvelous motivating psychology of desire for truth and the exercise of this desire for truth, will make life ever cleaner and happier, more rhythmical and artistic.

R. BUCKMINSTER FULLER
4D Timelock, Chicago, 1928, p. 28.

Preface

It is astounding the change in public attitude I have personally witnessed in my lifetime toward mental retardation. This was emphasized for me recently when the Vice President and I were visiting informally with a number of young couples at the home of a friend. During the evening the conversation turned to mental retardation. I found the young fathers and mothers unusually knowledgeable on the subject and one couple not at all reluctant to tell the group that they were parents of a retarded child.

What a change from the day when I was a young mother. Then we knew little about this handicap and we would have feared some social stigma or rejection had we discussed openly that we had a mentally retarded child. I am sure that every effort would have been made to conceal this fact.

When, today, I hear parents of retarded children say how fortunate they are to have those children now and not twenty or thirty years ago I know what they mean. For so much good has happened in such a brief time. Today the retarded who once were shunned by everyone—even in many cases by their relatives—find themselves the object of active interest by every segment of American life.

By the *scientists*, spurred by federal legislative programs, who are trying to learn more about the causes and the prevention of mental retardation. By the *medical profession*, which is demonstrating that good medical care, especially to the pregnant woman and the newborn child can prevent much retardation. By the *educators*, who are devising new and better ways to teach the retarded—and all youngsters, for that matter.

By the *recreation and physical training specialists*, who have discovered that their assistance, too, can make the retarded brighter and their lives more meaningful. By the *clergy*, who are learning that, armed with knowledge about mental retardation, they can offer solace and hope to the families and to these children—saving families and hopes that otherwise might be lost.

By the *businessman*, who is discovering that most of the retarded, when properly trained, can become valued employees—more productive at some tasks than those who do not have their limitations. By the *labor unions*, who are learning that the retarded can bring stability to some of their groups where membership was often transitory.

By the *political leaders* at all levels of government, who are learning that money invested in the prevention and improvement of mental retardation is a sound investment. And by the *young people* of America, the students in high schools and colleges. All of them— all of these segments of society—have shown their interest and concern in many ways.

MURIEL HUMPHREY

From the Keynote Address given at the Sixth Annual Conference on Mental Retardation, D. C. Children's Center.* Reproduced with permission.

* R.C. Orem and Guy Puntch, administrator at the D. C. Children's Center, coordinated the conference.

Acknowledgments

The editor acknowledges here his appreciation to the following individuals and groups. Mention of their names is not, of course, intended to imply that they endorse every point made in the book. But the editor has found discussion and correspondence with many of them helpful, and is grateful for their invitations to speak to the various Montessori schools, parent groups, and societies.

Dr. Willard Abraham, University of Arizona; David Adler, Principal, Wissahikan Elementary School and Past President, Children's House of Morristown, Pennsylvania; Dorothy Baumgartner; Korhan Berzeg; Mary Black; Dr. Brad Blanton, Capital Head Start; Dr. Judith Blanton, Economic Systems Corp.; Hugh Blocker, President, Montessori Children's House of Belair, Maryland; Virgil Burns, President, Montessori Foundation of Minnesota; Anne Byron, Directress, Children's House of Belair; Mrs. Loretta Clayton; Clinical Associates and Staff of the Optometric Extension Program; Dr. Russell Cort, Washington School of Psychiatry; Geraldine Cortese; Janet Darr; Jeanne Donovan; Ken Edelson, Editor, *Children's House*; Mother Isabel Eugenie, R.A., Directress, Montessori Teacher Training Center, Ravenhill Academy, Germantown, Pennsylvania; Dr. Urban Fleege, Associate Vice President, DePaul University; Dr. Richard Gitter; Gerald Gleeson, Jr., Member, Board of Education of Philadelphia, Pennsylvania; Earl Graham,[1] Editor of *Rehabilitation Literature*; Dr. Norris Haring, University of Washington; Nancy Hull; Tommy Johnson; Barbara Joniak; Mildred Kearney; Maria Kucinas; Mrs. Carl Liberti,

[1] For permission to reprint an abridged version of "Montessori Versus Orthodox," by Dr. William Argy, which appeared in the October, 1965, issue. © 1965, *Rehabilitation Literature*.

special education teacher, Neshaminy Schools; Dr. John Henry
Martin, Senior Vice President, Responsive Environments Corp.;
Margaret Mattis; Elliot McCleary,[2] Editor of *Today's Health*; Cleo
Monson, Executive Secretary, American Montessori Society;
Maryanne Moore, Assistant Directress, MTTC, Ravenhill Academy;
Nancy Moran; Margaret Morello; Margaret O'Dowd; Mrs. Mary
O'Hara,[3] Editor, *Harvard Educational Review*; Jon Osterkorn,
Executive Director, The Via Marsi Montessori School, Milwaukee,
for providing information about the school incorporated in the
book; Mary Plunkett; Mrs. Martin Ragsdale, President, Martin
Ragsdale, and membership of the Bucks County (Pa.) Montessori
Society; Mary Redcay; Sister St. Bernard, O.S.U., National Catholic
Kindergarten Association; Dr. Earl Shaefer, National Institutes of
Health; Mrs. G.F. Small, Editor, Illinois Montessori Society *News-
letter*; Staff of the D.C. Society for Crippled Children; Staff of the
Sylvan School; Keith Stanford; Sam and Dolores Telles; Rosemary
Thielke; Mrs. Raymond Tuman, Editor, Varnas Montessori Center
News of Chicago, and Staff of the Varnas Montessori Center; Dr.
J.E. Wallace Wallin; Watson Washburn, President, Reading Reform
Foundation; Mrs. Thomas Wilkes, New World Montessori School,
Oklahoma City; Peter Williamson, University of Pennsylvania.

The editor is most grateful to Mrs. Genevieve T. Alexander, outstanding Montessori headmistress in the Southwest, whose Lilliput
Schoolhouse operation (Corpus Christi, Texas) has generated, in
him, interest, inspiration, and insight.

[2] For permission to reprint excerpts from "The School Where Blind Children
See," which appeared in the February, 1967, issue. © 1967, *Today's Health*.
[3] For permission to reprint "Montessori and Piaget," by Dr. David Elkind,
which appeared in the Fall, 1967, issue. © 1967, *Harvard Educational Review*.

Foreword

THE PLAN OF THE BOOK

GENERAL CONSIDERATIONS

Throughout the book the editor has attempted to balance theory and practice, with general Montessori principles related to specific programs.

To broaden the reader's perspective, the Montessori method is discussed in terms of its past, present, and future.

Although it is not possible to detail in one book all the Montessori possibilities for special education, the various lines of exploration have been laid out, and the reader wishing to pursue further any of these lines is provided an extensive bibliography and suggested courses of action. For example, a parent who wants to learn more about Montessori will find helpful references to books and articles; also given are specific courses of action, so that he can become as involved in Montessori as he wishes.

The reader will notice that throughout the book Montessori in special education has not been treated as an isolated phenomenon; rather it has been presented against a comprehensive background of Montessori and regular education. Special education is but one dimension of regular education, for special children are, after all, on the same continuum with normal children.

THE FIVE SECTIONS AND APPENDIX

At the beginning of each section the reader will find a list of edited Montessori insights selected from an extensive review of books and articles by the Italian physician-educator.

Each set of insights is related to the material in the accompanying section and, taken as a whole, they provide an overview of the entire Montessori method.

Section I

In the Introduction, perhaps the major lesson to be learned from the Weber inventory of variant children is that lock-step, mass-production educational procedures are obsolete. The developmental needs of the huge population of special children, and all other children for that matter, can be met only by an individualized education, of which the Montessori approach provides an outstanding example, as seen by the chart that matches Montessori techniques with particular disabilities.

The brief history of the origins and development of the Montessori method traces Dr. Montessori's roots in special education, while noting her realization that normal children can benefit greatly from her "auto-education."

The various aspects of Montessori's life and work that are given illustrate their fundamental compatibility with the objectives and methods of many leaders in the field of special education today. But again, according to Montessori, her methods, which made possible the "miraculous" development of defective children, would produce even more remarkable results when applied to normal children.

Section II

In Section II it can be seen that in terms of theory and practice Montessori was well ahead of her time. It is only now, as behavioral scientists document the validity of her basic principles, that her work is beginning to gain widespread professional acceptance and institutionalization. As J. McV. Hunt has pointed out, Montessori's views at the turn of the century were too dissonant with three notions then in vogue (but since discredited): (1) intelligence is fixed, (2) development is predetermined, (3) early experience is not very important.

The pedagogical kinship of Fuller and Piaget with Montessori is described. Both of these men have supported the Montessori movement.

Section III

The Montessori method is comprised of three major parts: (1) motor, (2) sensory, and (3) intellectual (language, etc.) education. Dr. Richardson stresses the key role that sensory education plays in the Montessori classroom in building a solid foundation for abstract learning. Montessori summarized the matter in her observation that for the Montessori child touching becomes writing and looking becomes reading. Dr. Hendrickson notes, "Movement is the key to growth and development, to sensory inputs and motor outputs, to sensing, knowing and learning."

Lena Gitter, using the number rods as an example, shows how the child can teach himself abstract subjects through practice with concrete manipulatable Montessori materials.

Stevens points out that in view of the limited success of present-day methods for educating the deaf, it would appear most appropriate to examine the Montessori techniques for possible applications. It is worth noting that Alexander Graham Bell, a pioneer in deaf education, was one of Montessori's early friends in America.*

Dr. Datta describes many aspects of the Montessori approach that are of relevance to the slow-learning child, of whom there are several million in our schools.

Section IV

In Section IV are given practical examples of Montessori exercises, many of which can be adapted by public school teachers to their classrooms. Lena Gitter gives an example of a "real-life" Montessori project for retarded youngsters, and there are observations taken from Rosetta Rietz's classroom.

Dr. Dunn's detailed case history illustrates how Montessori education can complement therapy in the treatment of brain damage.

---

* *McClure's Magazine* introduced Montessori to American readers with a series of articles beginning in May, 1911. Editor Samuel S. McClure wrote in his autobiography: "Alexander Graham Bell, whose chief interest has always been in teaching and methods of teaching, although he is best known as inventor of the telephone, told me that he considered the introduction of the Montessori system in the United States as the most important work that *McClure's Magazine* had ever done." *My Autobiography*. New York, Stokes, 1914, p. 253.

Finally, there are brief accounts of some Montessori activities in three schools that serve special children.

Section V

Where does the Montessori method go from here? In Section V, two Montessori research studies are highlighted. Hopefully, there will be scores of such studies undertaken in the years immediately ahead.

Dr. Ofiesh and Dr. O'Keefe discuss the emerging educational technology, especially as it relates to culturally disadvantaged children—the largest single group of special children in the United States. This ingenious equipment is able to begin where the Montessori didactic apparatus ends.

The "Guide to Action," which offers specific steps for exploring and expanding Montessori, will be useful to parents, undergraduate and graduate students, and professionals.

Appendix A

Appendix A provides an edited summary of selected Montessori lectures to teachers of special children. As Dr. Richardson has noted, Montessori's notes on techniques for using her teaching or didactic material "are more detailed and precise than any other available today."

Contents

I

Introduction

INSIGHTS

1. Traditional education tends to exert a leveling, limiting influence; the child needs a new education featuring individualized methodology, self-teaching materials, and a new, indirect role for the teacher.

2. The usual classroom has lacked the "organization of work in freedom" necessary for autoeducation; the Montessori prepared environment offers a flexible format designed to aid human development.

3. The teacher, and other adults, can learn from observing the child how to assist him; the adult who forces unnecessary help upon the child hinders the child's self-development.

4. The environment at large, as well as that of the school, must be reformed; the new school will constitute, in effect, a "living laboratory" where pupils and teachers experiment.

5. Montessori education presupposes an active learner, who is motivated inwardly to form his personality and to make intellectual conquests.

6. It is the child's potential for autoeducation and inner discipline, not the Montessori method as such, that is responsible for the successful results of the Montessori indirect, individual approach to education.

7. In a spontaneous, expansive, active education, the natural drive of the child to self-development is aided by a secure, yet stimulating environment.

8. The extensive Montessori apparatus and activities provide a "cosmic curriculum" of three main parts: (1) systematic sensory education, (2) motor or muscular education (coordination, fitness,

etc.), and (3) intellectual and cultural development (language, math, creative expression, etc.).

9. The movable, Montessori materials, specifically designed to be chosen and manipulated by the young child, enable the child to absorb much abstract content inductively.

10. The Montessori method evolved from skilled observation by her and other teachers of children, using interesting materials in a prepared environment relatively free from interruptions.

11. Montessori's practical approach to teaching the language arts (listening, speaking, reading, writing) features multisensory materials, programmed preparation, and plentiful practice in practical application.

12. A disorderly environment interferes with learning and promotes insecurity; the child needs the opportunity to concentrate on tasks for considerable blocks of time.

13. It was the intense concentration of a child working with a piece of didactic material that encouraged Montessori to "plan out a special method for the education of children."

14. In the "liberty within limits" of the prepared environment, children are encouraged to develop and exercise self-discipline.

15. The concept of Montessori "autoeducation" involves self-teaching through interesting tasks with self-chosen didactic materials that have a built-in "control of error," which enables the child to correct his own mistakes.

Who is the special or exceptional child? Although terminology in the field of special education is still in the process of development, we can for our purposes define such a child as follows: one who deviates from normal physical, intellectual, emotional, or social patterns to a degree warranting special consideration.

Of course, a child may deviate in one or more of the above areas of human development, and in varying degrees at different times, and the special consideration can take many forms: special or augmented services, special classes or scheduling, etc.

Likewise, the deviation can be in a positive direction, as well as negative. For example, a child with superior intellect is exceptional.

Classifications of special or exceptional children vary widely with the purposes and criteria of the classifier. Weber's listing of variant children, who have an impairment or disadvantage that requires special consideration in the educative process, is more comprehensive than most such compilations.

Interestingly, Montessori believed that the standards we employ to gauge "normal" human development are misleading and really sub-normal. That is, given a scientific child-rearing coupled with a truly individualized education in a prepared environment, children would, she said, reveal new standards of development and achievement—new norms far above our present expectations.

WHO ARE THE VARIANT CHILDREN?

To our knowledge there is no comprehensive, up-to-date national inventory of children who are variously known as disabled learners, handicapped children, disadvantaged children, exceptional children, or variant children. The figures that exist are sometimes estimates and are often found in fragmented form. Moreover, there is little evidence of interagency and interassociation coordination with regard to the data or evidence that the data is being used meaningfully (*i.e.*, programmatically rather than for such purposes as fund raising).

Not all variant children are disabled learners, but most of them are in terms of the mass-production educational system with which they are confronted. Consider just a few of the difficulties: the dyslectic child has mechanical (*i.e.*, perceptual) problems; the child with ataxic cerebral palsy must curtail many of his activities; many children, such as the physically handicapped and the emotionally disturbed, suffer peer group nonacceptance or ridicule; children who are emotionally disturbed or who have congenital birth defects may be hospitalized for lengthy periods; and the children of the poor, to list only one of many problems, often suffer from severe nutritional deficiencies. None of these is conducive to learning and developing. However, in a greatly modified educational system, many millions of these children would respond and learn beautifully.

As noted earlier, only a small percentage of variant children are identified as needing special education and only a fraction of these actually receive it. Who are the millions of other variant children who have an impairment or disadvantage that interferes with the learning process? The following list, which is not exhaustive, provides gross estimates of the order of magnitude.

1. *Children of the poor.* Michael Harrington estimates that there are 22,000,000 persons under the age of eighteen living in poverty in the United States.[1] The vast majority of these are school-age children who are socially impaired (failure-oriented, stunted in growth, and damaged in personality).

2. *Brain-damaged children.* Estimates of the number of children with minimal brain damage run from 400,000 to 4,000,000.[2] However, when children with severe convulsive disorders, severe perceptual problems, and severe motor problems are added, the number probably increases by several million.

3. *Emotionally disturbed children.* The National Committee Against Mental Illness estimates that there are about 4,000,000 children under the age of fourteen who are in need of psychiatric care because of emotional difficulties. Some 500,000 to 1,000,000 of these children are so seriously disturbed that they require immediate psychiatric help. A number of references such as the National Association for Mental Health use the figure of 10 percent (over 5,000,000 children) of the total population as having "a mental or emotional disorder requiring psychiatric treatment."[3] However, these figures do not include those children whose emotional problems are not severe enough for them to be classified as "emotionally disturbed," but whose emotional problems nevertheless cause learning difficulties.

4. *Mentally retarded children.* Of America's estimated mentally retarded (now nearly 6,000,000 individuals), approximately 2,500,000 are children and young people under twenty years of age. Two million of these children are "mildly retarded," 150,000 are "moderately retarded," 100,000 are "severely retarded," and 50,000 are "profoundly retarded."[4]

The nation's retarded number three of every 100 live births.[5] Based on the 1964 live birth statistics, this means that every year approximately 126,000 are added to the already existing 6,000,000 retardates. However, these figures do not include that gray area between "certified mental retardation" and children whose IQ range (75 to 90) indicates low-normal coping abilities.

5. _Socially orphaned children_. Alvin Schorr, an investigator in the Office of Economic Opportunity, estimates that there are between 7,000,000 and 8,000,000 socially orphaned children in our nation (_i.e._, children who lack one or both parents).[6]

6. _Children with chronic diseases._ In the period July, 1959, through July, 1961, the National Health Survey found that an annual average of 13,996,000 chronic conditions were reported among children under the age of seventeen. (It must be noted here that these include hearing impairments.) The 13,996,000 conditions were distributed among 11,116,000 children, so that almost one child in every five under the age of seventeen (18 percent of the population in that age group) had at least one chronic condition.[7]

The rate of prevalence of hay fever, asthma, and all other allergies was 74.3 per 1,000 children (this figure projected for the entire school-age population becomes 4,160,800 children), and for sinusitis, bronchitis, and other respiratory diseases, 34.2 per 1,000 children under the age of seventeen. (This figure projected for the entire school-age population becomes 1,915,200 children.)[8]

The rate of prevalence of paralysis and orthopedic impairments was 26.3 per 1,000 children (this figure projected for the entire school-age population becomes 1,472,800 children), speech defects, 8.8 per 1,000 (this figure projected for the entire school-age population becomes 492,800 children), and heart disease, 4.2 per 1,000 (this figure projected for the entire school-age population becomes 235,200 children.)[9] Comparable, though slightly lower figures (extrapolated for the school-age population) are reported by the Public Health Service.[10]

7. _Children with visual impairments_. There are 10,200,000 children in need of eye care.[11] (This number projected to 1970 becomes 12,500,000.)[12] The prevalence rate of blindness among school-children is approximately 34 per 100,000 pupils enrolled (about

20,000). Actually, the true rate of blindness for this group is probably higher, since all legally blind schoolchildren are not registered with the American Printing House for the Blind, which compiled these statistics.[13] The New York Association for the Blind provides "a very conservative estimate" of 120,000 legally blind and partially seeing under twenty years of age. The association also emphasizes that this figure does not take into account children with crossed eyes, children needing glasses, and lesser, and usually unnoticed, visual impairments.

8. _Children with aural impairments_. It has been estimated that 1,500,000 schoolchildren have hearing impairments and that many children enter school with their hearing already impaired.[14] School health studies have indicated that about 7 percent (the extrapolation is approximately 4,000,000) of our children already have hearing loss when they enter school, that during the elementary years the rate may rise to about 9 percent (approximately 5,000,000) by the fifth grade, and that in secondary school, the rate will have risen to 12 percent (approximately 6,500,000).[15]

9. _Battered children_. A conservative estimate of the number of battered children (_i.e._, children who have been beaten, maimed, tortured, burned, and starved) has been made by H.G. Earl as being on the order of 10,000.[16] However, unofficial estimates place the figure at 200,000.

10. _Iatrogenically taught children_. Alvin Toffler computes the number of iatrogenically taught students at 3,000,000. He says that "three million youngsters have teachers who are so unbalanced they shouldn't be responsible for children."[17] He cites, as supporting evidence, the book by Joseph T. Shipley, _The Mentally Disturbed Teacher_ (Philadelphia, Chilton, 1961), and Louis Kaplan's study, _Mental Health and Human Relations in Education_ (New York, Harper, 1959).

Now, if reliable numbers were available, we could add to this list enormous numbers of:

· _Children of migratory workers whose education is sporadic._
· _Children whose familial patterns of geographical mobility result in a lack of continuity in education_ (_i.e._, high transfer rates in

school, often because of the inability of the family to pay the rent).
· *Incarcerated delinquents who experience institutionalization as iatrogenic.*
· *Children with speech defects.*
· *Children who are hospitalized for lengthy periods.*
· *Children who are the offspring of some 2,000,000 alcoholic wage earners.*[18]

It should be obvious to all that many of these children are being counted more than once and that it is very difficult—given the poor state of the art of diagnosis, inept record keeping, and the lack of comprehensive focus—to arrive at an accurate gross number of variant children in our country. Thus, there will be some skepticism that perhaps 45 percent of the school-age population—again, relative to an educational system of mass production—consists of variant children who are in need of special attention, individual attention, special education, and compensatory education. However, there is another side to that coin. While multiple counting reduces the gross number (by what factor, it is presently impossible to estimate), it also serves to emphasize the compound nature of the educational problem by illustrating that many variant children are multiple-problem children.

ROBERT E. WEBER

REFERENCES

[1] Michael Harrington, "The World of Poverty," *American Federationist* (April, 1966).

[2] E.F. Lehman and R.E. Hall, "Who Is This Child?" *American Education* (Washington, D.C., Office of Education, April, 1966).

[3] *New York Times*, April 24, 1966.

[4] *The Retarded Can Be Helped.* National Association for Retarded Children (booklet).

[5] Ron and Patricia Deutsch, "Diagnosis/Retarded," *Parents' Magazine* (March, 1966).

[6] Alvin L. Schorr, "Program for the Social Orphans," *New York Times Magazine*, March 13, 1966.

[7] *Health of Children of School Age*, Department of Health, Education and Welfare, Children's Bureau, Publication No. 427, 1964.

[8] *Ibid.*

[9] *Ibid.*

[10] *New York Times*, April 24, 1966.

[11] *Facts About Children's Bureau Programs*, Department of Health, Education and Welfare, Children's Bureau, 1965.

[12] *Health of Children of School Age.*

[13] E.M. Hatfield, "Causes of Blindness in School Children," *The Sight Saving Review*. National Society for the Prevention of Blindness, 1963.

[14] *Facts About Children's Bureau Programs.*

[15] *Health of Children of School Age.*

[16] H.G. Earl, "10,000 Children Battered and Starved," *Today's Health* (September, 1965).

[17] Alvin Toffler, "What Parents Can Do About 'Bad' Teachers," *Good Housekeeping* (February, 1966).

[18] *The Wall Street Journal*, April 19, 1966.

The chart that follows is designed to convey some idea of the range of Montessori applications to the vast field of special education. Of course, in reality the seven areas of special needs overlap; likewise the Montessori approaches, methods, and materials overlap. The information is arranged in discrete categories for convenience only.

Many special educators (and regular teachers) have been using some of these very concepts and techniques for years, while not necessarily labeling them "Montessori." As will be explained in later sections, the Montessori method itself has roots in the philosophy and work of individuals in many fields, especially in what has come to be known today as special education.

OVERVIEW OF MONTESSORI IN SPECIAL EDUCATION

CHILDREN MAY HAVE SPECIAL NEEDS IN ONE OR MORE OF THESE AREAS. A FEW TYPES OF PROBLEMS ARE GIVEN UNDER EACH AREA	SOME MONTESSORI-ORIENTED APPROACHES, METHODS, AND MATERIALS THAT HAVE PROVED HELPFUL
1. PHYSICAL visual impairment hearing impairment chronic health problems	multisensory approach to learning: visual, auditory, tactile, kinesthetic, etc. sensory education use of concrete materials "isolation of difficulty" in materials stimuli of sufficient intensity; analysis of sounds
	graded quantities and qualities of materials prepared environment development of child's latent capacities removal of obstacles to child's development elements of "science of child care" education as "aid to life" attention to child's formative period and physical development natural laws of development followed
2. PERCEPTUAL lack of perceptual proficiency	education for observation exercises to develop accuracy and speed in perception exercises in isolation of the senses practice in comparing and classifying use of the three-period lesson perceptual training linked with motor activity and language development child as explorer, making discoveries in his environment Children's House rich in sensory experience

CHILDREN'S NEEDS	MONTESSORI APPROACHES
3. MOTOR poor posture, coordination, dexterity, and motor skills	motor education; analysis of movements education for orderly movement exercises to improve breathing, walking, etc. development of positive body imagery mastery of movement; precision in movement liberty of pupil; work on floor furniture adapted to child's physique outdoor activity manual work creative arts manipulatable materials "exercises of practical life"
4. INTELLECTUAL difficulty with abstractions, limited powers of association, reasoning, judgment	sensorimotor education as foundation language fostered systematically concrete materials; bead math material much inductive learning brief, simple, clear lessons verbal stimuli not overemphasized simple-to-complex sequences much practice in making discriminations control of error in materials didactic objects as "materialized abstractions" reality-oriented education children learn from each other (three-year age span in class) repeating of exercises as needed

CHILDREN'S NEEDS	MONTESSORI APPROACHES
5. LANGUAGE AND COMMUNICATION difficulties in speech, reading, and writing	program of specific exercises for language development guiding of growth in language during early, formative years speech problems detected and worked with in preschool period teaching of exact vocabulary extensive preparation for writing and reading sandpaper letters, movable alphabets, and other materials employed child's "absorbent mind" and "sensitive period" for language acquisition exploited grammar taught early and indirectly children encouraged to communicate with each other and with teacher careful attention given to teacher's speech children stage little dramas
6. MOTIVATION negative attitudes history of failure	teaching of success preparation and practice leading to achievement cooperation, not competition child proceeds at own pace individuality respected satisfaction in work range of task difficulty patient teacher spontaneity encouraged confidence stemming from competence some mastery of environment gained intrinsic motivation

CHILDREN'S NEEDS	MONTESSORI APPROACHES
7. BEHAVIOR emotional and social maladjustment aggression; withdrawal	ground rules in environment liberty within limits discipline through activity habits of *work* and *order* encouraged normalization of child as goal concern for child's psychic life "cohesion in the social unit"—children help each other external organization aids internal order lesson of silence study of childhood mentality observation of individual child rational education to decrease psychic maladies self-discipline
8. PERSONAL— PERSEVERANCE limited grooming and self-care skills distractability	children helped to help themselves exercises to promote self-reliance independence encouraged interesting materials furnish motives of activity opportunity to complete cycles of activity nonintervention by teacher exercises in concentration "love of work" promoted self-direction

Dr. Mabel Talbot of Kent State University, in her treatise* on Seguin's systematically developed pedagogy, discusses Seguin's influence upon Montessori, who translated a copy of his book, reconstructed methods and materials described therein, and applied them to "idiot children." Montessori's pupils, taking state examinations, surpassed their normal peers.

"Dr. Montessori then did what Seguin had hoped might be done: she undertook to use and develop further the physiological method as a way of teaching normal children."

Montessori lived a long (1870–1952) and active life. Some of the formative experiences that influenced her education and training and shaped her many-faceted career are reviewed here, followed by brief descriptions of a number of these facets.

CONDENSED HISTORY OF THE ORIGINS AND DEVELOPMENT OF THE MONTESSORI METHOD

While assistant doctor at the Psychiatric Clinic of the University of Rome, and having turned her attention to the study of children's diseases, Montessori visited insane asylums to study the sick and to select subjects for the clinics. As an outgrowth of her interest in idiot children, who were at that time housed in the general insane asylums, she became conversant with the special method of education devised for them by Edouard Seguin. She was led to study thoroughly the idea, then beginning to be prevalent among physicians, of the efficacy of "pedagogical treatment" for various conditions such as idiocy. Pedagogy, it was felt, must join with medicine in the treatment of disease; but Montessori, however, believed that mental deficiency presented chiefly a *pedagogical*, rather than mainly a *medical*, problem.

* Mabel Talbot, *Edouard Seguin: A Study of an Educational Approach to the Treatment of Mentally Defective Children.* New York, Teacher's College, 1964, pp. 118–119.

She was called upon by the Minister of Education to deliver to the teachers of Rome a course of lectures on the education of feeble-minded children (an edited summary of selected lectures appears in Appendix A). This course soon developed into the State Ortho-phrenic School, which she directed for more than two years.

In this school was an all-day class of children composed of those from the elementary schools who were considered hopelessly deficient. Later, there was founded a Medical Pedagogic Institute, where, besides the children from the public schools, were brought together all of the idiot children from the insane asylums in Rome.

Montessori and her colleagues spent two years preparing the teachers of Rome for a special method of observation and education of feeble-minded children. After visiting London and Paris to study the education of deficients, she gave herself over completely to the actual teaching of the children, directing at the same time the work of the other teachers in her institute.

She was more than an elementary teacher, in the usual sense, being present, or directly teaching the children, from eight in the morning to seven in the evening without interruption. These two years of practice were Montessori's first and, as she put it, "my true degree in pedagogy." From the very beginning of her work with deficient children (1898 to 1900), she believed her methods were not limited to the instruction of such children, but contained educational principles more rational than others in use, so much more so, indeed, that through their means an inferior mentality would be able to grow and develop. This feeling, "so deep as to be in the nature of an intuition," became her controlling idea after she had left the school for deficients. *Slowly, Montessori became convinced that similar methods applied to normal children would set free or develop their personalities in a marvelous and surprising way.*

She undertook a thorough study of what was then known as remedial pedagogy, and, wishing to study normal pedagogy and the principles upon which it is based, registered as a student of philosophy at the university. "A great faith animated me, and although I did not know that I should ever be able to test the truth of my idea, I gave up every other occupation to deepen and broaden its conception. It was almost as if I prepared myself for an unknown mission."

According to Montessori, the methods for the education of deficients originated at the time of the French Revolution in the work of Jean Itard, a physician who pioneered the scientific study of diseases of the ear.

He attempted a methodical education of the sense of hearing, with experiments in the institute for deaf-mutes founded in Paris by Pereire. Later, having in charge for eight years the idiot boy known as "the wild boy of Aveyron," he extended to the treatment of all the senses those educational methods that had proved effective in the treatment of the sense of hearing. A student of Pinel, Itard was, in Montessori's words, "the first educator to practise the observation of the pupil in the way in which the sick are observed in the hospitals, especially those suffering from diseases of the nervous system."

Montessori considered Itard's written descriptions of educational efforts and experiences to be practically the first attempts at experimental psychology. But, she credits Edouard Seguin, "first a teacher and then a physician," with having completed a genuine educational system for deficient children. Seguin took the experiences of Itard as his starting point, applying these methods, modifying and completing them during a period of ten years' experience with children taken from the insane asylums and placed in a little Paris school. He described this work in a volume of more than six hundred pages, published in 1846: *Traitement Moral, Hygiène et Education des Idiots*. Later, Seguin emigrated to the United States, where he founded institutions for deficients, and after another twenty years of experience published the second edition of his book, under a very different title: *Idiocy and Its Treatment by the Physiological Method*. In it Seguin had carefully defined his method of education, calling it the physiological method, no longer referring in the title to a method for the "education of idiots" as if the method were special to them, but speaking now of idiocy treated by a physiological method.

After her study of the methods in use throughout Europe with deficient children, Montessori concluded her experiments upon the deficients of Rome and taught them for two years, following the writings of Seguin and Itard.

She then began new experiments that included an original method for the teaching of reading and writing, a part of the education of the child that she felt was inadequately treated in the works of both Itard and Seguin.

She succeeded in teaching a number of the "idiots" from the asylums to read and to write so well that she was able to present them at a public school for an examination together with normal children. *And they passed the examination successfully.*

These results were deemed "near miraculous" by some observers, but Montessori knew that the boys from the asylums had been able to compete with the normal children only because they had been taught in a different way. They had been helped in their psychic development, while the normal children had, instead, been suffocated, held back. She found herself thinking that if, someday, the special education that had developed these "idiot children" so remarkably could be applied to the development of normal children the "miracle" would no longer be possible. According to Montessori, "the abyss between the inferior mentality of the idiot and that of the normal brain can never be bridged if the normal child has reached his full development."

While others were admiring the progress of her deficients, she searched for the reasons that kept the happy, healthy children of the regular schools on so low a plane that they could be equaled in tests of intelligence by retarded pupils.

Having justified through experience her faith in Seguin's method, Montessori withdrew from active work among deficients and began a more thorough study of the works of Itard and Seguin. She translated into Italian and copied out by hand the writings of these men from beginning to end, "making for myself books as the old Benedictines used to do before the diffusion of printing," that she might weigh the sense of each word, and read the spirit of the author. When she had finished copying the 600 pages of Seguin's French volume she received a copy of his English book, published in 1866, and translated it with the help of an English friend. Seguin—the man who had studied abnormal children for thirty years—expressed the idea that the physiological method, which has as its base the individual study of the pupil and derives its educative methods from the analysis of physiological and psychological phenomena, must come also to be applied to normal children. This step, he believed, would show the way to a complete human regeneration.

To Montessori, the voice of Seguin "seemed to be like the voice of the forerunner crying in the wilderness," and her thoughts "were filled with the immensity and importance of a work which should be able to reform the school and education."

At this time she was registered at the university as a student of philosophy, taking courses in experimental psychology. At the same time she made researches in pedagogic anthropology in the elementary schools, studying the methods used for the education of normal children. This work led to the teaching of pedagogic anthropology in the University of Rome.

Montessori had long wished to experiment with the methods for deficients in a first elementary class of normal children. In late 1906, she was invited by the Director General of the Roman Association for Good Building to organize infant schools in its model tenements. His plan was to gather together in a large room all the little ones between the ages of three and seven belonging to the families living in the tenement. The play and work of these children was to be conducted under the guidance of a teacher who would have her own apartment in the tenement house. The first Casa dei Bambini or "Children's House" was opened on January 6, 1907, in the San Lorenzo district.

Montessori was thus given the opportunity to apply the methods used with deficients to normal children, not of elementary school age, but of the age usual in infant asylums.

If a parallel between the deficient and the normal child is possible, she felt it would be during the period of early infancy, "when the child who has not the force to develop and he who is not yet developed are in some ways alike."

Methods that made growth possible to the mental personality of the idiot should, according to Montessori, aid the development of young children, and should comprise a hygienic education of the entire personality. Many defects that become permanent, such as speech defects, the child acquires through being neglected during the vital period between three and six, the time when he forms and establishes his principal functions.

Wherein lies the significance of Montessori's pedagogical experiment in the "Children's Houses"? It represents, according to the Italian doctor, the results of a series of trials in the education of "normal" young children, with methods already used with deficients.

She considered her ten years of practical experiments as a summing up of the forty years of work done by Itard and Seguin. Her work, however, was not simply an application of their methods to young children, for, as in the case of the teaching of reading and writing, she developed her own methodology differing from that of Itard and Seguin.

R. C. OREM

SOME ASPECTS OF MARIA MONTESSORI OF PARTICULAR INTEREST TO SPECIAL EDUCATORS

Observer—herself a patient observer of children; trained teachers to observe; developed sensory education for children to develop their perceptual-motor and observational skills; observation the central element of the Montessori method.

Innovator—designed and invented much didactic and gymnastic equipment and apparatus for sensory, mathematics, language, and motor education; credited with introducing child-sized furniture into the classroom; developed pedagogical measuring instruments; utilized flexible schedules and groupings and "cosmic" curriculum for individualized education; Montessori method basically the opposite of traditional education.

Teacher—taught children of various ages, socioeconomic levels and "types" (retarded, culturally deprived, normal, etc.); conducted teacher-training course in various countries; held Chair of Pedagogic Anthropology at the University of Rome; opened first Casa dei Bambini (Children's House) in 1907.

Author—from 1912 to 1917 alone, five major books by her in English editions—*The Montessori Method* (1912), *Pedagogical Anthropology* (1913), *Dr. Montessori's Own Handbook* (1914), *Spontaneous Activity in Education* (1917), *The Montessori Elementary Material* (1917)— averaged 368 pages in length; authored some twenty texts and booklets now in English, plus dozens of articles, pamphlets, etc. *The Montessori Method*, her classic, an educational "best seller" in many parts of the world today.

Scientist—pioneering efforts to develop a science of education or scientific pedagogy; her concept of the teacher as experimenter, conducting research in the living laboratory of the classroom; ultimately concerned with the establishment of a science of child care; the Montessori method an interdisciplinary approach synthesizing biology, medicine, experimental psychology, psychometry, anthropology, and other fields.

Student—at age twenty-six, received with honors degree as Doctor of Medicine and Surgery at the University of Rome (the first woman to do so); a student of anthropologist Sergi; also studied the works of Seguin and Itard; graduate study in philosophy and other fields; Montessori, a lifelong student of the "child as teacher," also acknowledged learning much from the teachers she trained and observed.

Other—in addition, Montessori was a *traveler* and *lecturer*, spending periods of time in England, France, Holland, India, the United States, and other countries. She was also a *scholar*, whose *Montessori Method* contains references to the work of nearly fifty educators and scientists, while her *Pedagogical Anthropology* refers to some two hundred researchers in various disciplines. Finally, she was a *clinician*, serving as assistant doctor at the University Psychiatric Clinic, Director of the Medical Pedagogical Institute, and maintaining a private medical practice for several years.

Special educators have long found Montessori-type activities useful. Working with children who present an awesome range of physical, intellectual, emotional, and social disabilities, such teachers must, like Montessori, be observant, experimental, and innovative to be effective.

What is not sometimes recognized is that normal children need teachers with these same qualities, at least as much as their special peers, if the learning environment is to be optimum. They too need exposure to a prepared environment, organized with challenging materials, and guidance by a "teacher as programmer." Because they do not have sensory, intellectual, or other deficits, many normal children are able to learn in spite of ineffective teaching in the regular program.

Most of the following points, then, have direct implications for regular education *in addition to* special education. *Montessori principles, in effect, serve as a bridge uniting the two.*

SOME ASPECTS OF THE MONTESSORI METHOD OF PARTICULAR RELEVANCE TO SPECIAL EDUCATION, YET OF GENERAL SIGNIFICANCE TO REGULAR EDUCATION

1. *Medico-biological orientation.* Montessori, trained as a physician, was concerned with the "whole child," his total development and physical well-being. She was interested in the child's diet, exercise, and mental health, as well as his intellectual and social development.

2. *Rooted in the work of early leaders in special education.* Montessori was greatly influenced by the work of French physician-educator Jean Itard, who taught deaf-mutes (and was himself a student of Pinel—a pioneer in psychology); Edouard Seguin, another French physician-educator and student of Itard, likewise exerted great influence upon Montessori, who, for example, translated his works into Italian, including his 600-page French volume.

3. *Montessori early a teacher of special children.* She became interested in "idiot children" while assistant doctor at the University Psychiatric Clinic, and studied children's diseases. She taught a course on educating the feeble-minded child to Rome teachers, then formed and directed the State Orthophrenic School. She taught idiot children at the Medical Pedagogic Institute for two years ("from

~~eight in the morning to seven in the evening without interruption"~~)
and also directed the work of the other institute teachers.

4. *Montessori studied the methods of special education employed in Europe and America.* In addition to studying the writings of the special educators of her day, she traveled widely to study the then-current practices for the teaching of deaf-mutes and other "deficient children" in London, Paris, and elsewhere. This experience enabled her to observe first-hand the effectiveness of these practices, and is reflected in the comprehensiveness of her own methodology.

5. *Observation fundamental to the method.* Montessori spoke of observation as a form of pedagogy. With the teacher trained to observe carefully, and with a physician attached to the "Children's House" as recommended by Montessori, the classroom becomes a diagnostic environment.

The Montessori teacher is in a unique position to observe such aspects of the child as his physical, perceptual-motor, and speech development and to take appropriate action (remedial instruction, parent conference, referral, etc.) when a problem is noted.

6. *Prepared environment to provide security and promote interest in learning.* The child is free to move and work within an atmosphere of order, made possible by ground rules and absorbing didactic materials.

The didactic material and ground rules of the Montessori environment provide a flexible structure and "organization of work" enabling children to occupy themselves constructively in relative freedom.

A Montessori class, even with special children, may be considerably larger than a traditional one, and yet function more effectively. The children can immerse themselves in the materials and exercises that furnish the "motive of activity," as Montessori termed their allure.

The "ground rules" protect each child's work from the disruption of other children. The long blocks of time enable the child to concentrate upon a particular task for as long as he wants.

7. *Self-help and independence encouraged.* Through such activities as those Montessori termed "Exercises of Practical Life" the child learns to care for his person and his environment. The Montessori

child does not have to rely upon someone else to comb his hair, polish his shoes, or sweep the floor. He develops pride in his own grooming and dress, and in doing his share to maintain an attractive environment.

8. *A milieu of cooperation, not competition.* In the Montessori system, emphasis is upon the intrinsic reward of self-development rather than upon prizes and punishments. A child is free to help another, if invited by that child. The typical age range of three years in a class offers the advantages of a nongraded situation. The older children can directly help the younger, or the latter may learn simply by watching their older classmates.

Montessori children admire each other's work. They share responsibility for "schoolkeeping" tasks and can work in large or small groups as circumstances dictate.

9. *Careful attention given to language development.* In Montessori's unified approach to language development, the importance of the earliest "formative" years for absorbing language is recognized, and the "sensitive periods" for reading and writing are utilized. There are materials and exercises designed to impart and improve skills in listening, speaking, reading, and writing.

10. *Focus upon the individual.* The child can work directly with the didactic material he has chosen, at his own pace, for long, uninterrupted periods of time, while the teacher moves about the room to observe and give individual lessons as needed.

The schedule for each child is flexible, dictated by his interests and needs and not imposed from without. No two children need follow the same curriculum. Each displays his own unique pattern of potentials and progress. The individual follows the lead of his own "inner teacher."

11. *Teaching of success, not failure.* Children who may have suffered considerable failure in other settings are afforded the opportunity to experience success in a Montessori classroom. The child can begin with simple basic tasks that match his current level of competence, and gradually—step by step—lead to mastery of ever-more-challenging exercises.

Much of the material contains what Montessori termed "control of error." That is, the child can recognize immediately when he has made an error, and is able to try an alternative response without waiting for the teacher to help him.

12. *Abundance of concrete, manipulatable material.* The child can exercise his sense of touch fully with the large selection of readily available materials that enable him to learn intuitively various principles and rules of mathematics, language, science, etc. He can move to the more complex, abstract exercises after sufficient practice and preparation.

Much of the material was originally developed by Montessori in her experiments with deficient children.

13. *Opportunity for repetition and practice.* The young learner needs time to repeat an activity until he has mastered it. Montessori spoke of the child's "love of repetition." It was, in fact, her observation of a child working with wooden blocks and cylinders that inspired her to "plan out a special method for the education of children."

She recognized that each learner proceeds at his own unique pace, and therefore requires an environment in which he is neither pressured ahead nor held back by the performance of his peers.

14. *Opportunity to move as one learns.* The children can move about the room to explore and can lay out their work on the carpeted floor, rather than be confined to desks.

There are many large and small muscle exercises to aid motor coordination.

The emphasis is upon active learning and "active" inner discipline rather than passivity and external discipline.

15. *Sensory education for perceptual proficiency.* There are specific materials and exercises to improve the child's sensory abilities: seeing, hearing, touching, etc. The child is encouraged to make ever-finer sensory discriminations involving colors, sizes, shapes, sounds, textures, etc., as he concurrently learns a precise vocabulary —*e.g.*, "long, longer, longest."

Many special children with a sensory problem can benefit from the Montessori materials and methods, which were often originally developed with deficient children.

The child is encouraged to discover his environment by touching it.

The materials may be said to progress from "the concrete to the abstract." At each stage in the learning process the child is preparing for the next, more challenging, task. Piaget and other researchers have shown how important early extensive motor experience is in the development of the higher mental processes.

16. *Multisensory approach to learning.* With the didactic materials and exercises, the child can apply several senses to a particular learning task. He is not limited, say, to a verbal approach. For example, with the sandpaper letters, he can feel (tactile), trace (stereognostic), see (visual), and hear (auditory) the letter as the teacher pronounces it. One sense can reinforce another in the learning situation. A child who favors a particular style or mode of learning (motor type, visual type, etc.) has the opportunity to express this preference.

17. *Normal development fostered early.* Montessori stressed the vital importance of the early "formative" years in the child's development. The "prepared environment" is conducive to exposing problems of a developmental nature in their early stages, while they may yet be remediated. It thus serves as a diagnostic environment.

The child from birth to age six passes through a series of what Montessori termed "sensitive periods." There is, for example, a sensitive period for learning languages. Rather than waiting until the child is six to begin reading instruction, the Montessori directress informally exposes the child at age three to sandpaper letters, the movable alphabet, etc., to guide language development. The young child's "absorbent mind" possesses a remarkable capacity for indirect learning.

II

Montessori, Fuller, and Piaget

INSIGHTS

1. The child's mental development is marked by "sensitive periods" —times when a particular type of learning is most readily acquired. These times of "creative sensitivity" are but one manifestation of the child's great inner powers.

2. The child may be likened to a psychic embryo containing potentialities in the form of "directing tendencies" leading to the development of a unique individual personality.

3. During the child's "formative period" from birth to about age six, many defects may be acquired in language, etc., if proper attention and aid are not given to his development.

4. Sensory education lays a foundation for the development of reason. The child learns to make progressively refined discriminations, judgments, decisions.

5. There are definite stages in the various areas of the child's development: physical, emotional, intellectual, social, and spiritual.

6. The environment must be prepared to meet the needs of the child at each stage of every area.

7. The child's "miraculous" ability to master language without formal instruction is proof enough of his capacity for autoeducation —self-teaching. The child's "absorbent mind" enables him to take in language directly from the environment.

8. Movement is vital to mental development; the Montessori child is allowed to move as he learns.

9. Motor or muscular education is designed to help the child learn to move and act in coordinated, efficient fashion.

10. To be most effective, education must begin at birth and assist the child as he is forming himself in interaction with the environment.

This chart tends to confirm the notion that the Montessori philosophy and methodology are in remarkable accord with much of current educational theorizing and practice. In his earlier A Montessori Handbook *and* Montessori for the Disadvantaged, *the present editor assembled detailed evidence to show the basic compatibility of Montessori's work with that of leading contemporary behavioral scientists: B.S. Bloom, J. Bruner, M. Deutsch, D. Hebb, W. Fowler, H. Harlow, J. McV. Hunt, O.K. Moore, B.F. Skinner, W.G. Walter, and R. White, among others.*

Work in language learning, early reading, cognitive development, programmed learning, sensory and cultural deprivation, the psychology of motivation, and many other fields is "zeroing in" on the critical importance of the child's earliest years for growth and development— and demonstrating the relevance of the Montessori approach to early childhood education.

MONTESSORI—THE ANTICIPATOR

"NEW" CONCEPTS AND TRENDS IN THE 1960'S	MONTESSORI APPLICATIONS SIXTY YEARS AGO
educational revolution	Montessori "New Education," basically the opposite of traditional education
interest in education of culturally deprived	first Children's House opened in Rome slum
Head Start enrollment at age four or five	enrollment at age three or even below
Child Development Center	first "Casa dei Bambini" (Children's House) opened in 1907
"responsive environment"	prepared environment
school as community center	first Children's House in apartment tenement—teacher lived in apartment
community involvement in school	Children's House as property of the parents
interest in physical and mental well-being of "whole child"	a physician attached to each Children's House
health examinations and follow-up—medical, dental, psychological, etc.	school conceived as diagnostic environment preventive approach
interest in nutrition and its effect upon learning	a large part of child's diet entrusted to the school staff
innovation	school as experimental laboratory
child-centered education	student self-choice, self-pacing, self-development
human development	education as aid to life
functional architecture and furnishings	Children's House as "the best for the child"
light, functional furniture	Montessori generally credited with introduction of children's furniture
learning booths, carrels	each child has private work space, with access to cabinets and shelves of books and materials
new learning games, kits, models	1,400 pieces of didactic material developed for various subjects

"NEW" CONCEPTS AND TRENDS IN THE 1960'S	MONTESSORI APPLICATIONS SIXTY YEARS AGO
programmed learning "autotelic activity"	"autoeducation" through "control of error" in sequential didactic material
curriculum development	"cosmic curriculum"
early reading	children reading and writing by five
revitalized teacher education	Montessori training for "new teachers"
use of paraprofessionals, teacher aides, etc.	Montessori's first teacher a teen-age girl who lacked traditional teacher training
team teaching	children teach each other—"team learning"
new teacher roles—*i.e.*, less lecturing	teacher as experimenter indirect teaching
development of improved tests	Montessori devised her own tests and measurements
ungraded primary	three-year age span in class
flexible grouping	children themselves free to choose to work alone or in small groups
flexible scheduling	long blocks of uninterrupted time provided
individualized instruction	teacher trained as observer
less emphasis upon marks and grades	reduction of external rewards and punishments learning as its own reward
greater student responsibilities	student self-discipline
language stimulation	utilize "sensitive period" for language learning, and child's "absorbent mind" teacher as language exemplar children allowed to talk
provision for sensorimotor learning	sensory and motor education
learning how to learn	"education from birth"
utilize intrinsic motivation in learning process	child teaches himself much of the time; follows "inner teacher"
foster joy of discovery in learning	child seen as explorer making discoveries in environment

Maria Montessori was described in an American newspaper of her day as "an authentic educational genius," and "the most interesting woman in Europe." R. Buckminster Fuller, in a recent issue of Time *magazine, was called "the greatest living genius of industrial-technical realization in building . . . an anticipator of the world to come."*

Forty years ago he prophesied the emergence of a system of spontaneous education of choice for children, "similar to the Montessori System," as noted in the quotation at the beginning of this book. Today, the Fuller geodesic domes, which in recent years have covered more square feet of the earth than any other single kind of shelter, are proving to be the ideal enclosure for the "prepared environment" for child rearing and "autoeducation."

FULLER, MONTESSORI, AND THE CHILD

It has been said of Richard Buckminster Fuller (by astronomer Harlow Shapley): "I suppose that he is the brightest man alive."*

INTRODUCTION

One who reads the various books and articles by and about R. Buckminster "Bucky" Fuller and Maria Montessori will note a number of striking parallels between the Fuller pedagogy and that expounded in the Montessori literature.

R. Buckminster Fuller

The manifold accomplishments of Bucky Fuller in half a dozen fields are a separate story. In fact, there have already been two

* News Release, American Medical Association: "Bucky" Fuller's Views To Be Heard by U. S. Medicine. Keynote speech, National Congress on Environmental Health Management conducted by the AMA, New York City, April 24–26, 1967.

biographies* detailing his varied contributions to man's progress, and there will in all likelihood be more. Lately, he has been the subject of a *Time* cover story, a *New Yorker* profile, a *New York Times Magazine* feature, and the author of a series of articles in *Saturday Review.*

Fuller, holder of a dozen honorary doctorates, has lectured and conducted courses and seminars at some 200 colleges and universities around the world. His inventions, or "realizations" as he prefers to call them, include the Dymaxion house, the Dymaxion car, and the geodesic dome. (The American Pavilion at EXPO '67 in Montreal was a huge geodesic dome.) Fuller's Dymaxion map was the first cartographic projection system to be granted a U.S. patent.

Author of many books (*Nine Chains to the Moon, The Unfinished Epic of Industrialization,* etc.), he was Charles Eliot Norton Professor at Harvard in 1961-1962. At present, he is professor of design science at Southern Illinois University.

Maria Montessori

It might be well to repeat here a few of Maria Montessori's accomplishments.

At twenty-six years of age she received a "double honors degree" as Doctor of Medicine and Doctor of Surgery (the first woman to do so) from the University of Rome—where, for a period of time, she held the Chair of Anthropology.

Her interest in institutionalized children led to her appointment by the Minister of Education to deliver a course on the education of retarded children to Italian teachers, culminating in the formation of the State Orthophrenic School, which she directed for over two years.

The director general of the Roman Association for Good Building, which owned more than 1,400 tenements in Rome, invited her to organize infant schools in its model tenements. The first Casa dei Bambini was opened on January 6, 1907.

* R.W. Marks, *The Dymaxion World of Buckminster Fuller.* Carbondale, Ill., Southern Illinois University Press, 1960; and John McHale, *R. Buckminster Fuller* ("Makers of Contemporary Architecture" Series). New York, G. Braziller, 1962.

⁓ She developed a wide variety of didactic materials for the teaching of language, mathematics, and other subjects, and is generally credited with the introduction of child-sized furniture into the classroom. ⁓

In a five-year period, 1912 to 1917, five books by Montessori appeared in English.

She conducted a number of international training courses, helped found schools patterned on her educational principles in various parts of the world, and wrote additional books before her death, in 1952.

The editor has selected and organized a number of quotations that illustrate the basic compatibility in thinking between Montessori and Fuller—two great educational figures of the twentieth century.

TEXT

New Education Needed

Both Fuller and Montessori have noted the fundamental inadequacy of traditional education. Says Fuller:

> What usually happens in the educational process is that the faculties are dulled, overloaded, stuffed and paralyzed, so that by the time most people are mature, they have lost use of many of their innate capabilities.[1]

Montessori asks: "Is there anything more immovable, stagnant, and indifferent than the education of today?"[2]—a question not likely to win the endearments of traditional educationalists. "The educational methods now in use," she says, "proceed on lines exactly the reverse of ours."[3]

Fuller's long-time hope is that "we may soon begin to realize what we are doing and may alter the 'education' process in such a way as to help the new life to demonstrate some of its very powerful innate capabilities."[4]

Montessori says that "not only must the teacher be transformed, but the school environment must be changed."[5]

Autoeducation

Speaking of the child's powers of self-development, she says: "I believe that the work of the educator consists primarily in protecting the powers and directing them without disturbing them in their expansion."[6]

In her *Education for a New World*, Montessori adds: "Faced with this vision of great power in the child and of its importance to humanity, we must observe that power minutely, and see in what way we can help it."[7]

Importance of Observation

Both Fuller's and Montessori's works are the result of exquisitely acute observation, and these great teachers counsel all those who would "educate" to first learn to observe.

"Man," says Fuller, "can only do what nature permits him to do. Man does not invent anything. He makes discoveries of principles operative in nature and often finds ways of generalizing these principles and reapplying them in surprise directions. That is called invention."[8]

Montessori notes that "if we study the history of discoveries, we will find that they have come from *real objective observation* and *from logical thought*. These are simple things, but rarely found in one man."[9]

The new education, according to Fuller, will be concerned "primarily with exploring to discover not only more about the universe and its history but about what the universe is trying to do, about why man is part of it, and about how man may best function in universal evolution."[10]

New Teacher

The "new teacher" will be, above all else, an observer. Says Montessori: "The study of the individual should suggest to us the particular method of education required by him."[11] She notes that "our only book should be the living individual; all the rest taken together form only the necessary means for reading it."[12] Furthermore, "actual training and practice are necessary to fit for this method teachers who have not been prepared for scientific observation,"[13] and "it is remarkable how clearly *individual differences* show themselves, if we proceed in this way; the child, conscious and free, reveals himself."[14]

Individualized Education

Fuller, too, envisions a truly individualized educational process:

> Real education, however, will be something to which individuals will discipline themselves spontaneously under the stimulus of their own ticker-tapes—their individually unique chromosomes. Everyone has his own chromosomal pattern. No two persons have the same appetite at the same time. There is no reason why everyone should be interested in the geography of Venezuela on the same day and hour unless there is some "news" event there, such as a revolution. However, most of us are going to be interested in the geography of Venezuela at some time—our own time—but not all on the same day. Simultaneous curricula are obsolete. We must make all this information immediately available (over the two-way TV's), ready for the different individual human chromosomal ticker-tapes to call for it.[15]

Montessori emphasizes the importance of individual interests, which can be accommodated in a prepared environment:

> There is no fixed program or schedule which directs the children's activities, nor does the directress hold herself to any fixed plan for the day's work. The child has already reached a certain plane of development and as he enters the room he does not enter lacking interest. He is neither ready nor resigned to submit to the work which a teacher has prepared for him and his companions. On the contrary he enters possessed of a definite interest.[16]

Concentration as the Key

The child unquestionably has powers of concentration that traditional education has failed to tap. The typical schoolroom is simply not designed to free these powers.

Says Fuller, who visited with Einstein:

I am quite confident that I can say with authority that Einstein, when he wanted to study, didn't sit in the middle of a school room. That is probably the poorest place he could have gone to study. When an individual is really thinking, he is tremendously isolated. He may manage to isolate himself in Grand Central Station, but it is despite the environment rather than because of it.[17]

Fuller writes that he has "taken photographs of my grand-children looking at television. Without consideration of the 'value,' the actual concentration of a child on the message which is coming to him is fabulous. They really 'latch on.' "[18]

Montessori observes that "a child who is interested in what he is doing goes on and on without fatigue, but when the teacher makes him change every few minutes and rest, he loses interest and gets fatigued."[19] The adult "ought to offer the child that which is necessary for his internal life, and leave him free to produce."[20]

Prepared Environment

"Very seriously," says Fuller, "much of what goes on in our schools is strictly related to social experiences, and that is fine—that's good for the kids. But I would say we are going to add much more in the very near future by taking advantage of the children's ability to show us what they need."[21]

Montessori would agree: ". . . we have merely set the child free, and helped him to 'live.' It is he who has taught us 'how' the child lives, and what other needs he has besides his material wants."[22]

The greatest need of the child is an environment within which he can find the means for his full human development.

"It is not enough to nourish their bodies; they are hungry for intellectual food,"[23] says Montessori. ". . . The child's love of *knowledge* is such that it surpasses every other love. . . ."[24]

Fuller has noted that even the very young child is not only capable of but motivated to process information from the world around him:

I will say that it is very clear to me that when a child stands up, breathing and co-ordinating all these complex patterns by himself, gets his own balance and starts drinking in the patterns of cosmos and earth he is apparently spontaneously interested in co-ordinating the total information—the total stimulation. He craves to understand —to comprehend. That is why he asks his myriad questions.[25]

Montessori refers to language as a good example of the young child's creative absorptive mentality: "By merely 'living' and without any conscious effort the individual absorbs from the environment even a complex cultural achievement like language."[26]

Cosmos as Curriculum

According to Fuller, the child's capability must be challenged by a "cosmic curriculum."

> Our whole educational process, all the way up from the elementary school, is one of taking the child who has an innate, comprehensive, co-ordinate capability (not only to teach itself to walk but to be interested in the heavens) and give him differentiated parts—elements to work with. The prime patrons of the planetariums and the like are the children, because they are spontaneously interested in the universe, that is, in the comprehensive rather than in the specialty— the elements. We get them to school, and we say forget the universe, and we give them A, B, and C.[27]

Montessori says: "Since it has been seen to be necessary to give so much to the child, let us give him a vision of the whole universe."[28]

Reality in Education

Says Fuller:
"I've made tests with children—you have to get them right away, before they take in too many myths. I've made a paper model of a man and glued him down with his feet to a globe of the world, and put a light at one side, and shown them how the man's shadow lengthens as the globe turns, until finally he's completely in the shadow. If you show that to children, they never see it any other way, and they can really understand how the earth revolves the sun out of sight."[29]

The Montessori method could be termed reality-oriented: "Education must prepare the modern child for the renewed civilization of our day, this civilization which is based upon positive research of truth; that is, the child whose hand, whose eye, and whose ear are eager to grasp the truth with precision, and who becomes capable of mental concentration."[30]

Elsewhere, she says that "children . . . must be shown complete pictures of reality, which vividly suggest fact and situation."[31]

Both Fuller and Montessori acknowledge the profound effect of environment upon the individual.

Wrote Montessori in *Spontaneous Activity in Education*:

> That which holds good of all living beings—that the individual cannot be divorced from his environment—is more profoundly true in its application to psychic life, because the content of environment, constituting the means of auto-experience which evolves man, is an essential part of him, and, indeed, is the individual himself.[32]

Says Fuller: "I made up my mind at this point that I would never try to reform man—that's much too difficult. What I would do was to try to modify the environment in such a way as to get man moving in preferred directions. It's like the principle of a ship's rudder. . . ."[33]

For Fuller and his thousands of students and associates around the world, 1965–1975 is World Design Science Decade. He proposes that all the universities around the world be encouraged to invest the next ten years in a continuing study of how to make the total world's resources, which now serve only 43 percent, serve 100 percent of humanity through competent complex design science.

Like Montessori, Fuller has unreserved trust in the potential of his students for mastery of their environment.

> It should be emphasized here that the overall planning and ultimate success of the "World Design Science Decade" rests with the world students' initiative, encouraged and assisted by their schools, universities, and professional organizations.[34]

SUMMARY

A comparison of selected works of R. Buckminster Fuller and Maria Montessori reveals many areas of basic agreement.

Both recognize the need for an educational revolution if the child's inherent potentials for self-development and "autoeducation" are to be realized.

They stress the critical importance of exquisitely acute observation by the "new teacher." The teacher must skillfully prepare an "individualized" environment to foster expression of each child's powers, such as his power of concentration.

Fuller and Montessori note that the child, if given the opportunity by a respectful adult, can teach the adult much, including what the child's unique needs are.

Finally, this pair of educators observe that the child's powerful motivation to process information demands a greatly expanded curriculum. The world and the child's curriculum are, in reality, one.*

REFERENCES

[1] R. Buckminster Fuller, *Education Automation* (Carbondale, Ill., Southern Illinois University Press, 1962), p. 12.

[2] Maria Montessori, *The Absorbent Mind*, 3rd ed. (Adyar, Madras 20, India, Theosophical Publishing House, 1961), p. 13.

[3] ———, *Spontaneous Activity in Education* (New York, Stokes, 1917), p. 207.

[4] R. Buckminster Fuller, *Education Automation*, p. 12.

[5] Maria Montessori, *Spontaneous Activity in Education*, p. 142.

[6] *Ibid.*, p. 194.

[7] Maria Montessori, *Education for a New World* (Adyar, Madras 20, India, Kalakshetra Pub., 1959), p. 12.

[8] R. Buckminster Fuller, *Education Automation*, pp. 52–53.

* For further reading, see: R. Buckminster Fuller, "The Design of Recreative Human Environments" in *Montessori for the Disadvantaged*, R.C. Orem, ed. New York, Putnam's, 1967; and "Emergent Man—His Environment and Education" in *The Case for Early Reading*, by George L. Stevens and R.C. Orem. St. Louis, Warren H. Green, Publisher, 1967.

⁹ Maria Montessori, *The Montessori Method* (New York, Stokes, 1912), p. 254.

¹⁰ R. Buckminster Fuller, *Education Automation*, p. 43.

¹¹ Maria Montessori, *Pedagogical Anthropology* (New York, Stokes, 1913), p. 444.

¹² *Ibid.*, p. 26.

¹³ Maria Montessori, *The Montessori Method*, p. 88.

¹⁴ *Ibid.*, p. 95.

¹⁵ R. Buckminster Fuller, *Education Automation*, p. 15.

¹⁶ Maria Montessori, "Organization of Intellectual Work in School," *Journal of Proceedings and Addresses*. NEA, Vol. 53, 1918, p. 718.

¹⁷ R. Buckminster Fuller, *Education Automation*, p. 35.

¹⁸ *Ibid.*, p. 36.

¹⁹ Maria Montessori, *Education for a New World*, p. 67.

²⁰ ———, *Spontaneous Activity in Education*, p. 275.

²¹ R. Buckminster Fuller, *Education Automation*, p. 36.

²² Maria Montessori, *Spontaneous Activity in Education*, p. 324.

²³ *Ibid.*, p. 323.

²⁴ ———, *The Montessori Method*, p. 118.

²⁵ R. Buckminster Fuller, *Education Automation*, p. 83.

²⁶ Maria Montessori, *The Formation of Man* (Adyar, Madras 20, India, Theosophical Pub. House, 1955), p. 87.

²⁷ R. Buckminster Fuller, *Education Automation*, p. 69.

²⁸ Maria Montessori, *To Educate the Human Potential* (Adyar, Madras 20, India, Kalakshetra Pub., 1956), p. 8.

²⁹ R. Buckminster Fuller, quoted in "Profile," by Calvin Tomkins, *The New Yorker* (Jan. 8, 1966).

³⁰ Maria Montessori, "Education in Relation to the Imagination of the Little Child," *Journal of Proceedings and Addresses*. NEA, Vol. 53, 1918, pp. 666–667.

³¹ ———, *The Montessori Elementary Material* (New York, Stokes, 1917), p. 199.

³² Maria Montessori, *Spontaneous Activity in Education*, p. 113.

³³ R. Buckminster Fuller, quoted in "Profile," *The New Yorker*.

³⁴ ———, *Education Automation*, p. 78.

David Elkind "was involved in research using a Piagetian framework when Piaget was still just a name to many American psychologists."* Elkind spent the year 1964–1965 with Piaget in Geneva.

Of all contemporary scientists, Swiss psychologist Jean Piaget has probably done the most important research into how the child learns to think. In the UNESCO publication Education and Mental Health, *reference is made to the Montessori type of activity pursued by Piaget's subjects. It is not surprising to learn that for years he has been President of the Swiss Montessori Society.*

PIAGET AND MONTESSORI †

Unquestionably, the most impressive figure in the field of cognitive development today is Jean Piaget. We and the generations that follow us will be grateful for his pioneering work.**

In recent years there has been a renaissance of American interest in the work of two Europeans, Jean Piaget and Maria Montessori. Although the reasons for this rebirth of interest are many and varied, there are two that appear beyond dispute. First of all, both Piaget and Montessori have observed hitherto unexpected and unknown facets of child thought and behavior. Secondly, and in this lies their impact, both these innovators have formulated the general laws and principles of child thought and behavior implicit in their observations. In the case of Piaget these observations led to a new philosophy of knowledge, while in the case of Montessori they led to a new philosophy of education.

Unfortunately, it is not possible in a presentation such as this to do justice to the contributions of these two innovators. Under the

* Review by Irving Siegel in *Contemporary Psychology*, August, 1968, of *Jean Piaget: Six Psychological Studies*, edited by David Elkind. New York, Random House, 1968.

† This selection appeared in the Fall, 1967, *Harvard Educational Review* and is reprinted here with permission.

** Jerome S. Bruner, *Toward a Theory of Instruction*. Cambridge, Massachusetts, Harvard University Press, 1966, pp. 6–7.

circumstances all that I would like to do is describe, and illustrate with research data, three original ideas about child thought and behavior that Piaget and Montessori arrived at independently but share in common. Before turning to those ideas, however, it seems appropriate, by way of introduction, to note some of the parallels and divergences in the Piagetian and Montessorian approaches to child study.

PARALLELS AND DIVERGENCES

Among the many parallels between the work of Piaget and Montessori one of the most pervasive is the predominantly biological orientation they take toward the thought and behavior of the child. This is not surprising in view of their backgrounds. Piaget, for example, was publishing papers in biology while still in his teens, and took his doctorate in biology at the University of Lausanne. Likewise, Montessori was trained as a physician and engaged in and published medical research (cf. Standing, 1957). This shared biological orientation is important because both these workers see mental growth as an extension of biological growth and as governed by the same principles and laws.

In addition to, and perhaps because of, this shared biological orientation, both Piaget and Montessori emphasize the normative aspects of child behavior and development, as opposed to the individual differences aspect. Piaget, for example, has been concerned with identifying those mental structures that, if they hold true for the individual, also hold true for the species. Likewise, Montessori has been concerned with those needs and abilities that are common to all children, such as the "sensitive periods" and the "explosions" into exploration. This is not to say that Piaget and Montessori in any way deny or minimize the importance of individual differences; far from it. What they do argue is that an understanding of normal development is a necessary starting point for a full understanding of differences between individuals.

The third parallel in the approaches of Piaget and Montessori is one of personality. Both these workers manifest what might be called a *genius for empathy with the child*. When reading Piaget or Montessori, one often has the uncanny feeling that they are somehow able to get inside the child and know exactly what he is thinking and feeling, and why he is doing what he is doing at any given moment. It is this genius for empathy with the child that, it seems to me, gives their observations and insights—even without the buttressing of systematic research—the solid ring of truth.

Despite these parallels, Piaget and Montessori also diverge in significant ways in their approaches to the child. For Piaget, the study of the child is really a means to an end rather than an end in itself. He is not so much concerned with children *qua* children as he is with using the study of the child to answer questions about the nature and origin of knowledge. Piaget is in no way callous toward the child, and has given not a little of his considerable energies and administrative talents to national and international endeavors on the part of children; but he has not concerned himself with child-rearing practices, and only recently and with reluctance has he dealt with educational issues (*e.g.*, Piaget, 1964). There is only so much any one person can do, and Piaget sees his contribution primarily in the area of logic and epistemology and only secondarily in the area of child psychology and education.

Montessori, on the other hand, was from the very outset of her career directly concerned with the welfare of the child. Much of her long and productive life was devoted to the training of teachers, the education of parents, and the liberation of the child from a pedagogy that she believed was as detrimental to his mental growth as poor diet was to his physical growth. Montessori was dedicated to improving the lot of the child in very concrete ways.

The other major divergencies between these two innovators stem more or less directly from this central difference in approach. Piaget is primarily concerned with theory while Montessori's commitment was to practice. Moreover, Piaget sees his work as being in opposition to "armchair" epistemology and views himself as the "man in the middle" between the archempiricists and the archnativists. Montessori, in contrast, saw herself in opposition to traditional Herbartian pedagogy, which she regarded as medieval in its total disregard for the rights and needs of the child.

With this brief introduction by way of parallels and divergences as a starting point, we can now turn to some of those ideas about the child that Piaget and Montessori share in common. If I focus upon Montessori's ideas rather than her methods, it is because that is where the convergence of Piaget and Montessori is greatest and where the available research is most relevant. Definitive research with respect to the effectiveness of Montessori's methods seems, insofar as I have been able to determine, yet to be completed.

CONVERGING IDEAS

Nature and Nurture

It would be easy, but unfair and incorrect, to contrast Piaget and Montessori with those who seem to take a strong environmentalist position with respect to mental development. Even if we start with writers at the extreme end of the environmentalist camp, such as Watson (1928) or more recently, Bruner (1960), it would be a misrepresentation to say that they deny the role of nature in development. The real issue is not one of either nature or nurture but rather one of the character of their interaction. One of the innovations of Piaget and Montessori lies, then, not so much in their championing of the role of nature as in the original way in which they have conceived the character of nature-nurture interaction.

As was mentioned earlier, both Piaget and Montessori see mental growth as an extension of physical growth, and it is in the elaboration of this idea that they have made their unique contribution to the problem of nature-nurture interaction. In their view, the environment provides nourishment for the growth of mental structures just as it does for the growth of physical organs. In addition, and this has been stressed particularly by Montessori, some forms of environmental nourishment are more beneficial than others for sustaining mental growth, just as some foods are more beneficial than others for sustaining physical growth. The "prepared environment" in the Montessori school is designed to provide the best possible nourishment for mental growth.

The relation between nature and nurture in mental growth is, however, not as one-sided as that. Not only does the child utilize environmental stimuli to nourish his own growth but growth must adapt and modify itself in accordance with the particular environment within which it takes place. Of the many possible languages a child can learn, he learns the one to which he is exposed. The same holds true for his concepts and percepts, which are, in part at least, determined by the social and physical milieu in which he grows up. Both Piaget and Montessori recognize and take account of this directive role that the environment plays in the determination of mental content. Indeed, the beauty of the Montessori materials is the way in which they simultaneously provide the child with nourishment for the growth of mental capacities and relevant educational content. In short, for both Piaget and Montessori, nature interacts in a dual way with nurture. As far as mental capacities are concerned, the environment serves as nourishment for the growth of mental structures or abilities whose pattern of development follows a course that is laid down in the genes. On the other hand, insofar as the content of thought is concerned, nature plays a more directive role and determines the particular language, concepts, percepts, and values that the child will acquire.

What evidence do we have for this conception of the dual character of nature-nurture interaction? With respect to the environment as a provider of nourishment for an inner-directed pattern of structural development, there is considerable evidence from Piaget-related research. In a study by Hyde (1959) children of different nationalities (including British, Arab, Indian, and Somali youngsters) were given a battery of Piaget-type number and quantity tasks. Regardless of nationality and language, these children gave the same responses as Piaget had attained with Swiss children. More recently, Goodnow and Bethon (1966) found little difference between Chinese and American children with respect to the age at which they manifested concrete reasoning. These cross-cultural findings suggest that children can utilize whatever stimuli are available in their immediate environs to foster their mental growth, just as children all over the world can utilize quite different diets to realize their physical growth.

At the same time, there is also considerable evidence with respect to the directive role that environmental stimulation plays with respect to the content of thought. In a cross-cultural study by Lambert and Klineberg (1967), for example, there were differences even at the six-year-old level in response to the question "What are you?" Most American children thought of themselves primarily as "a boy" or as "a girl," while Bantu youngsters usually described themselves in terms of race. Furthermore, Lebanese children frequently responded to the question in kinship terms and gave responses such as "the nephew of Ali." This study amply illustrates the role of the physical and social environment in shaping the child's self concept.

For both Piaget and Montessori, then, nature-nurture interaction has a dual character. In the case of mental capacities, nature plays the directive role and nurture is subservient, while just the reverse is true with respect to the content of thought. It is in their emphasis upon the dual character of nature-nurture interaction that Piaget and Montessori have made their signal contribution to this age-old problem.

Capacity and Learning

Within experimental psychology, the child is generally viewed as a naïve organism. That is to say, a child is one who is lacking in experience, although his capacity to learn is no different from that of the adult. If differences between children and adults exist, then they reside in the fact that adults have had more opportunity and time to profit from experience than have children. For both Piaget and Montessori, however, the child is a *young* organism, which means that his needs and capacities are quite different from those of the adult. This issue can be put more directly by saying that, for the experimental psychologist, capacity is determined by learning, whereas for the developmental psychologist, learning is determined by capacity or development.

To make this point concrete, let me use a crude but useful analogy. Over the past ten years we have seen several "generations" of computers. The early computers were relatively slow and quite limited in the amount of information they could store. The most recent computers, on the other hand, are extremely fast and have enormous memories. Even the earliest computers, however, could handle some of the programs that the high-speed computers can. On the other hand, no matter how many programs were run on the early computers, their capacity was not altered but remained fixed by the limits of their hardware. To be sure, by ingenious programming these early computers were able to do some extraordinary things, but their limitations in terms of hardware persisted.

As you have anticipated, the several generations of computers can be likened to the several stages in the development of intelligence. Just as the hardware of the computer determines its memory and speed, so the mental structures at any given level of development determine the limits of the child's learning. Likewise, just as the number of programs run on a computer leaves its speed and memory unaltered, so the number of problems a child has solved or the number of his concepts does not change his problem-solving or concept-learning capacities. Furthermore, just as we can, with elaborate programming, get the computer to do things it was not intended to do, so we can, with specialized training, get children to learn things that seem beyond their ken. Such training does not, however, change their capacity to learn any more than an ingenious computer program alters the speed or memory of the computer. This is what Piaget and Montessori have in mind by the notion that capacity determines learning and not the reverse.

This idea is frequently misunderstood by many advocates of Piaget and Montessori. Indeed, much of the acceptance of Piaget and Montessori in America today seems to be based on the promise their ideas hold out for accelerating growth. Nothing, however, could be further from their own beliefs and intentions. Piaget was recently quoted as saying, "probably the organization of operations has an optimal time. . . . for example, we know that it takes nine to twelve months before babies develop the notion that an object is still there even when a screen is placed in front of it. Now kittens go through the same stages as children, all the same substages, but they do it in three months—so they are six months ahead of babies. Is this an advantage or isn't it? We can certainly see our answer in one sense. The kitten is not going to go much further. The child has taken longer, but he is capable of going further, so it seems to me that the nine months probably were not for nothing." (Jennings,

1967, p. 82.) In the same vein, Montessori wrote, "We must not, therefore, set ourselves the educational problem of seeking means whereby to organize the internal personality of the child and develop his characteristics: the sole problem is that of offering the child the necessary nourishment." (Montessori, 1964, p. 70.)

The view that capacity determines what will be learned has been supported in a negative way by the failure of many experiments designed to train children on Piaget-type reasoning tasks (*e.g.*, Greco, 1959; Smedslund, 1959; Wohlwill, 1959; 1960). In addition, however, there is also evidence of a positive sort that substantiates the role of capacity in the determination of what is learned. In one of our studies, for example, we demonstrated that while six-, seven-, and eight-year-old children could all improve their perceptual performance as a result of training it was also true that the oldest children made the most improvement with the least training. (Elkind, Koegler, and Go, 1962.) We have, moreover, recently shown (Elkind, Van Doorninck, and Schwarz, 1967) that there are some concepts that kindergarten children cannot attain but which are easily acquired by second-grade youngsters. In the same vein, we have also demonstrated that there are marked differences in the conceptual strategies employed by children and adolescents and that these strategies limit the kinds of concepts that elementary school children can attain (Elkind, 1966; Elkind, Barocas, and Johnsen*; Elkind, Barocas, and Rosenthal*). Similar findings have been reported by Weir (1964) and by Peel (1960).

There is, then, evidence that capacity does determine what is learned and how it is learned. Such findings do not deny that children "learn to learn" or that at any age they can learn techniques that enable them to use their abilities more effectively. All that such studies argue is that development sets limits as to what can be learned at any particular point in the child's life. These studies are in keeping with the positions of Piaget and Montessori. As we have seen, neither of these innovators advocates the acceleration of mental growth. What they do emphasize is the necessity of providing the child with the settings and stimuli that will free any given child to

* Submitted (see References).

realize his capacities at his own time and pace. Such a standpoint is quite different from one that advocates the acceleration of mental growth.

Cognitive Needs and Repetitive Behavior

One of the features of cognitive growth that Piaget and Montessori observed, and to which they both attached considerable importance, is the frequently repetitive character of behaviors associated with emerging mental abilities. Piaget and Montessori are almost unique in this regard since, within both psychology and education, repetitive behavior is often described pejoratively as "rote learning" or "perseveration." Indeed, the popular view is that repetition is bad and should be avoided in our dealings with children.

What both Piaget and Montessori have recognized, however, is the very great role that repetitive behavior plays in mental growth. In his classic work on the origins of intelligence in infants, Piaget (1952a) illustrates in remarkable detail the role that primary, secondary, and tertiary circular reactions play in the construction of intellectual schemas. Likewise, Piaget (1952b) has pointed out the adaptive significance of children's repetitive "Why?" at a later age. Such questions, which often seem stupid or annoying to adults, are in fact the manifestation of the child's efforts at differentiating between psychological and physical causality.

Montessori has likewise recognized the inner significance of repetitive behavior in what she calls the "polarization of attention." Here is a striking example with which, I am sure, many of you are familiar:

"I watched the child intently without disturbing her at first, and began to count how many times she repeated the exercise; then, seeing that she was continuing for a long time, I picked up the little armchair in which she was seated and placed chair and child upon the table; the little creature hastily caught up her case of insets, laid it across the arms of the chair and gathering the cylinders into her lap, set to work again. Then I called upon the children to sing; they sang, but the little girl continued undisturbed, repeating her exercise even after the short song had come to an end. I counted

forty-four repetitions; when at last she ceased, it was quite independently of any surrounding stimuli which might have distracted
her, and she looked around with a satisfied air, almost as if awakening
from a refreshing nap." (Montessori, 1964, pp. 67–88.)

The role of repetitive behavior in intellectual development is not
extraordinary when we view mental growth as analogous to physical
growth. Repetitive behavior is the bench mark of maturing physical
abilities. The infant who is learning to walk constantly pulls himself
into an erect position. Later, as a toddler, he begins pulling and
dropping everything within reach. Such behavior does not derive
from an innate perversity or drive toward destruction, but rather
comes of a need to practice the ability to hold and to let go. What
the child is doing in such a situation is practicing or perfecting
emerging motor abilities. Mental abilities are realized in the same
way. In the course of being constituted, intellectual abilities seek to
exercise themselves on whatever stimuli are available. The four-
year-old who is constantly comparing the size of his portions with
those of his siblings is not being selfish or paranoid. On the contrary,
he is spontaneously exercising his capacity to make quantitative
comparisons. The Montessori child who repeatedly buttons and
unbuttons or replaces inserts into their proper holes is likewise
exercising emerging mental abilities. Piaget and Montessori see such
repetitive behaviors as having tremendous value for the child and as
essential to the full realization of the child's intelligence.

Although there is not a great deal of research evidence relevant
to the role of repetition in mental growth, I would like to cite some
findings from one of our studies which points in this direction. In
this study (Elkind and Weiss, 1967) we showed kindergarten,
first-, second- and third-grade children a card with eighteen pictures
pasted upon it in the shape of a triangle. The children's task was
simply to name every picture on the card. The kindergarten children
named the pictures according to the triangular pattern in which the
pictures were pasted. That is to say, they began at the apex and
worked around the three sides of the triangle. This same triangular
pattern of exploration was employed by third-grade children and
to some extent by second-grade children. First-grade children and
some second-grade youngsters, however, did a peculiar thing. *They*

read the pictures across the triangle from top to bottom and from left to right.

Why did the first-grade children read the pictures in this clearly inefficient way? The answer, it seems to me, lies in the fact that these children were in the process of learning the top-to-bottom and left-to-right swing that is essential in reading English. Because they had not entirely mastered this swing, they spontaneously practiced it even where it was inappropriate. Viewed in this way, their behavior was far from being stupid, and the same can be said for older slow-reading children who read the pictures in the same manner as the first-graders.

These findings thus support the arguments of Piaget and Montessori regarding the adaptive significance of repetitive behavior in children. Repetitive behavior in the child is frequently the outward manifestation of an emerging cognitive ability and the need to realize that ability through action. It was the genius of Piaget and Montessori that saw, in such repetitive behaviors as sucking and putting insets into holes, not stupidity, but rather intelligence unfolding.

SUMMARY AND CONCLUSION

I have tried to describe and illustrate with research data, three original ideas about child thought and behavior that Piaget and Montessori arrived at independently but which they share in common. The first idea is that nature and nurture interact in a dual way. With respect to the growth of abilities, nature provides the pattern and the time schedule of its unfolding while nurture provides the nourishment for the realization of this pattern. When we turn to the content of thought, however, just the reverse is true and nurture determines what will be learned while nature provides the prerequisite capacities. A second idea has to do with capacity and learning. For both Piaget and Montessori, capacity sets the limits for learning, and capacity changes at its own rate and according to its own time schedule. Finally, the third idea is that repetitive behavior is the external manifestation of cognitive growth and expresses the need of emerging cognitive abilities to realize themselves through action.

Before closing, I would like to say that the recent acceptance of Piagetian and Montessorian concepts in this country is gratifying and long overdue. It would be a great loss if within a few years these ideas were again to be shelved because they failed to accomplish what they were never designed to achieve. To avoid that eventuality, we need to try to accept Piaget and Montessori on their own terms and not force their ideas into our existing conceptual frameworks, or distort them for our own pragmatic purposes. Only in this way can we hope to gain lasting benefit from the outstanding contributions that Piaget and Montessori have made to the study of the child.

DAVID ELKIND

BIBLIOGRAPHICAL REFERENCES

Bruner, J.S., *The Process of Education*. Cambridge, Mass., Harvard University Press, 1960.

Elkind, D., Barocas, R.B., and Johnsen, P.H., "Concept Production in Children and Adolescents." *Journal of Educational Psychology* (submitted).

Elkind, D., Barocas, R.B., and Rosenthal, R., "Concept Production in Slow and Average Readers." *Journal of Educational Psychology* (submitted).

Elkind, D., Koegler, R.R., and Go, Elsie, "Effects of Perceptual Training at Three Age Levels." *Science*, Vol. 137 (1962), pp. 755–756.

Elkind, D., and Weiss, Jutta, "Studies in Perceptual Development III: Perceptual Exploration." *Child Development*. Vol. 38 (1967), pp. 553–561.

Goodnow, Jacqueline J., and Bethon, G., "Piaget's Tasks: The Effects of Schooling and Intelligence." *Child Development*. Vol. 37 (1966), pp. 573–582.

Greco, P., *"L'Apprentissage dans une Situation à Structure Opératoire Concrete: Les Inversions Successives de l'Ordre Linéaire Pare des Rotations de 180°,"* in J. Piaget, ed., *Etudes d'Épistémologie Génétique*, Volume 8. Paris, Presses Universitaires de France, 1959, pp. 68–182.

Hyde, D.M., "An Investigation of Piaget's Theories of the Development of the Concept of Number." Unpublished doctoral dissertation, University of London, 1959.

Jennings, F.G., "Jean Piaget: Notes on Learning." *Saturday Review*, (May 20, 1967), p. 82.

Lambert, W.E., and Klineberg, Otto, *Children's Views of Foreign Peoples*. New York, Appleton–Century–Crofts, 1967.

Montessori, Maria, *Spontaneous Activity in Education*. Cambridge, Mass.: Robert Bentley, 1964.

Peel, E.A., *The Pupil's Thinking*. London, Oldhourne Press, 1960.

Piaget, J., "Development and Learning," in R.E. Ripple and V.N. Rockcastle, eds., *Piaget Rediscovered*. Ithaca, N.Y., Cornell University School of Education, 1964, pp. 7–20.

———, *The Language and Thought of the Child*. London, Routledge & Kegan Paul, 1952 (b).

———, *The Origins of Intelligence in Children*. New York, International Universities Press, 1952 (a).

Smedslund, J., "*Apprentissage des Notions de la Conservation et de la Transitivité du Poids*," in J. Piaget, ed., *Etudes d'Épistémologie Génétique*, Volume 9. Paris, Presses Universitaires de France, 1959, pp. 85–124.

Standing, E.M., *Maria Montessori*. Fresno, Academy Library Guild, 1957.

Watson, J.B., *Psychological Care of Infant and Child*. New York, Norton, 1928.

Weir, M.W., "Developmental Changes in Problem Solving Strategies." *Psychological Review*, Vol. 71 (1964), pp. 473–490.

Wohlwill, J.F., "*Un Essai l'Apprentissage dans le Domaine de la Conservation du Nombre*," in J. Piaget, ed., *Etudes d'Épistémologie Génétique*, Volume 9. Paris, Presses Universitaires de France, 1959, pp. 125–135.

———, "A Study of the Development of the Number Concept by Scalogram Analysis." *Journal of Genetic Psychology*, Vol. 97 (1960), pp. 345–377.

MONTESSORI ACTIVITIES AND APPARATUS IN SPECIAL EDUCATION

Although the array of Montessori materials and exercises can be classified in various series and sequences, the editor has used a five-topic arrangement to outline the system: I—Exercises of Practical Life; II—Sensorial Materials and Exercises; III—Preparation for and Progress in Writing, Reading, Mathematics; IV—Creative Expression; and V—"Cultural Input." Under each of the five major topics are grouped representative examples of activities and/or apparatus which the editor has seen being used with special children of various types in Montessori schools and programs.

I. *Exercises of practical life*

Grooming and care of one's person

washing hands
combing hair
brushing teeth
cleaning and polishing shoes
brushing and hanging up clothes
dressing and undressing
buttoning, zipping, snapping, lacing, etc.

Helping to maintain order and attractiveness in one's environment indoors

sweeping
dusting
cleaning and waxing floor
cleaning and waxing furniture
polishing metal objects (brass, silver, etc.)
cleaning windows, mirrors, pictures
cutting and arranging flowers

Working outdoors

weeding
lawn care
raking
planting
watering plants
care and feeding of animals, fowl
picking fruit and gathering vegetables

Activities centering on snacks and meals
 washing and preparing vegetables, cutting, slicing, paring, etc.
 pouring, stirring, mixing, etc.
 setting the table
 serving at table
 eating, drinking, use of utensils, napkin, etc.
 clearing the table
 washing, drying, and putting away dishes

Etiquette and social relations
 receiving visitors
 offering assistance
 entering and leaving a room
 giving thanks
 asking permission
 apologizing
 telephone courtesy
 not disturbing others, or their work

Motor coordination and control
 sitting down and rising quietly
 good posture when standing
 walking, without bumping against people or furniture
 walking on line
 silence game
 lifting
 carrying furniture, alone and with others
 climbing
 dressing frames
 sorting, stacking, inserting, matching, tying, etc.
 using scissors, art materials, writing implements

Exercises with water and other liquids
 pouring, filling containers, changing water in flower vases,
  washing, soaking, rinsing, wringing, etc.

Exercises in carrying
 carrying jugs, glassware, basin, chairs, rolled-up carpet, etc.

Exercises in folding

folding tablecloths, napkins, newly-ironed linen, etc.

Exercises in opening and closing

opening and closing, quietly, room doors, cupboard and closet doors, windows, drawers, cabinets, etc.

II. *Sensorial materials and exercises*

1. *Visual*

   pink tower
   broad stair
   long stair
   solid wooden insets
   knobless cylinders
   geometric cabinet
   constructive triangles
   color tablets

2. *Auditory*

   sound boxes
   bells
   exercises with a watch

3. *Tactile*

   touch boards
   touch tablets
   collection of materials (silk, wool, etc.)
   collection of grains (rice, corn, etc.)

4. *Olfactory*

   smelling boxes and jars

5. *Gustatory* (taste)

   taste bottles (sweet, salt, acidic, etc.)

6. *Combined senses*

> thermic bottles and tablets
> baric tablets
> stereognostic exercises
> geometric solids
> binomial and trinomial cubes
> mystery bag

III. *Preparation for and progress in writing, reading, mathematics*

> plane insets
> metal insets
> sandpaper letters and numbers
> movable alphabet
> various geometric forms
> phonogram materials
> word games
> concrete objects
> grammar symbols
> reading analysis
> language cards, definitions, nomenclature
> reading and writing: words, sentences, stories
> numerical rods
> counting sticks
> card and bead material for decimal system
> boards and charts for: addition, subtraction, multiplication, division

IV. *Creative expression*

> paper cutting, pasting
> making colored designs with insets
> didactic material for music
> free-hand drawing
> painting
> clay modeling
> reading and writing poetry and prose
> dramatics

V. *"Cultural input"*

charts, cards, puzzles, maps, models

time-lines, books, etc., for such subjects as history, geography, botany, zoology

This system of activities and apparatus can help the special child (within the limits of his potential) in such ways as the following:

1. provide necessary order and structure
2. improve motor behavior, coordination, body imagery
3. improve perceptual functioning: perception of time, space, form, texture, size, and other dimensions
4. increase independence through acquisition of self-care skills
5. arouse and hold learner's attention, and develop his concentration
6. develop social skills, deportment, and self-discipline
7. improve language reception (listening, reading) and expression (speaking, writing)
8. develop habits of order and work

Of course, schools and education programs, whether they be Montessori or other, do not operate in isolation. As the special (and normal) child passes from infancy to adulthood, he displays physical, emotional, intellectual, social, and spiritual needs at the various developmental levels. Ideally, there will be responsive educational and training programs at the preschool, elementary, secondary, and higher education levels.

But the home, church, clinic, and community at large, as well as the school, must respond with coordinated programs to enhance the child's mental and physical health, self image, recreational and vocational skills, citizenship, and spiritual resources.

III

Montessori — A Sensorimotor
Approach to Special Education

III

INSIGHTS

1. The three-part Montessori method includes education of the senses, which employs a systematic methodology and materials; the other parts are motor or muscular education, and intellectual education, which features language development.

2. Education of the senses or sensory education is interwoven with language development; for example, when the child is learning to differentiate the length of rods he is concurrently learning a precise vocabulary: small, smaller, smallest, etc.

3. Stages in the education of the senses include: (1) recognition of identities, (2) recognition of contrasts, and (3) ever-finer discriminations involving very similar qualities and dimensions.

4. The didactic material, which Montessori developed in experiments with children, can be thought of as "materialized abstractions"; that is, the materials provide, in an orderly manner, standards of form, size, weight, color, texture, etc., against which the child can measure his observations and perceptions.

5. The child may learn to use a piece of the material by having the teacher give him a presentation or explanation, or he may learn by watching her instruct others; or he may learn simply by watching other children who have already learned to use it. He may, as Montessori put it, "experiment with intelligent modifications," but he is not allowed to abuse or damage the material, and he must return it ready for the next user when he is finished with it.

6. The child needs to move as he learns, and he needs to learn coordination of his movements. Features of the prepared environment such as carpeted work space on the floor, exercises of practical life, and light, movable furniture encourage movement.

7. Montessori believed that the teacher should assist the child to

follow his own natural laws of development; the teacher should be concerned that the child receives an adequate diet essential for healthy development.

8. Montessori used the term "normalized" to describe a child who has been freed in a secure, yet stimulating environment to function normally; the "deviated" child has suffered distortions of or departures from normal development.

For forty years, the staff and associates of the Optometric Extension Program, a nonprofit foundation for education and research in vision, have been performing significant research and related services in the field of human growth and development. From the work of the Child Care Section, for example, has evolved a clinical philosophy of developmental visual care and guidance that assists the child, whether "retarded," "normal," or "superior," in the integration of his entire visuomotor complex.

As is stressed throughout this book, Montessori recognized the crucial importance of abundant sensorimotor activity in primary learning; she developed multisensory materials enabling the child to accumulate information through sensorimotor manipulation. Dr. Benjamin Spock and Mildred Hathaway have noted in Redbook *(March, 1967):*

> Montessori materials were designed so that when used in the proper sequence they gradually lead children, over a period of several years, into an understanding of abstract ideas with a minimum of adult explanation and interference.

VISION DEVELOPMENT AND LEARNING

... childhood ... a sort of apprenticeship of the senses.*

Most of what one learns, once the skill of reading has been acquired, comes through the eyes, utilizing the process of vision. The *importance* of vision and its adequate development in all children, as a requisite for learning, would seem to be self-evident.

Vision is a process that includes the ability, among others, to look at marks on paper (symbols) that stand for a thing and allow one to know what that object feels like, sounds like, tastes like, smells like, or looks like, without actually feeling, listening to, tasting, smelling, or looking at the object. "Vision and visual perception are the end result of all other developments, not the starting point. If they were the starting point, every infant would fully understand everything he saw following the moment of birth. There would be no need for the long involved learning processes. Neither would there be the need for the long periods of infancy and childhood in which to learn."[1]

Vision is much more than an ability to see clearly at a distance and near (20/20 acuity). Vision includes the ability to know distances without pacing them off or measuring them; to know sizes and shapes without feeling things; to know the positions of things in space, the relation of one object to another, and up, down, sideways. Vision is learned and developed. The learning is done by the infant and child and no one teaches him. But conditions can be so arranged by parents and teachers that the learning takes place optimally, at the most appropriate time during the period of growth and maturation when the learning should occur. We are concerned here with the sequence, the stages of the abilities learned in the development of vision and the relationships to learning. We are also vitally concerned

* Jean Itard, *The Wild Boy of Aveyron.* New York, Appleton–Century–Crofts, 1962, p. 27.

with the conditions to be arranged to allow the child to develop the best possible visual process.

The stages of development of vision are the same for all children, be they so-called normal children, special, gifted, exceptional, or retarded. The time and timing is different for each child and can be different in each stage. Emphasis of activity at any one level or stage of development depends on the needs of the child for learning certain skills. Development of abilities in the latter stages is dependent on abilities acquired at earlier stages. Inadequate experiences at earlier stages can result in inadequate skills at higher levels. Hence, the learning of adequate abilities at every stage, in sequence, is essential to efficient visual functioning, for adequate visual perception, learning, and achievement in our culture.

The human system is arranged for the purpose of movement and the detection of movement. Movement is the key to growth and development, to sensory inputs and motor outputs, to sensing, knowing, and learning. Dr. Montessori stated, "Movement is therefore the essential to life . . . for it is precisely the characteristic which distinguishes not only man, but all the animal kingdom from the vegetable world."[2] "Motility is the seedbed of the mind."[3] It has been said that if it (information or experience) doesn't get into the muscle it doesn't get into the brain. And the potential for storage of information in the brain is tremendous. The ten billion neurons of the human cortex are estimated to have a potential number of connections approaching 10^{278} (10 followed by 278 zeros). The circuitry is developed and established by movement, movement in all the systems and subsystems of the human. The circuitry loop consists of afferent (input) on-and-off patterned impulses from sense organs (eyes, ears, etc., as well as muscles, joints, etc.) and efferent (output) on-and-off impulses to muscles to produce movement. Then there are feedback circuits that fold back on the original inputs to modify and confirm them.

"Each eye transmits as much information to the brain as does all the rest of the body. It can send a million impulses per milli-second. For the whole organism including eyes, the input has a maximum of three million signals per milli-second."[4] This means three billion impulses per second arrive in the cortex and central nervous system.

Of these, two billion come from the two eyes, about one billion from each eye each second. Those from the two eyes must be matched with each other to form a composite or single perception of the world seen. The patterns from eyes must in turn be matched with the inputs from the rest of the body, other sense organs, muscle systems, etc. Thus, any interference between the matching of the two eyes (inputs) can create interference in the data processing by the brain, restrict and interfere with the search for meaning, and the efficiency of control of movement.

STAGES OF DEVELOPMENT

How and in what order does the infant, and later the child, develop these patterns of movement? Skeffington,[5] in his programs of continuing education for optometrists, has proposed four areas of observation of development, four stages of movement development through which the infant and child can be seen to progress. His model shows *vision* to be an emergent or derivative of these four areas of performance, each system and subsystem contributing to the ultimate skill of comprehending the information that reaches the organism from the environment through its light receptors, the eyes.

"First, the infant wages a contest with gravity."[6] The *first* area of performance observed and considered is one of total body movement, for locomotion, exploring, and organizing himself within his environment. The mechanisms of balance (the labyrinths of the inner ear, proprioception from the muscles and joints, and about 20 percent of the impulses from eyes) feed information to the brain, where appropriate areas originate and dispatch orders for movement to maintain balance and equilibrium with gravity. The patterning of these inputs is practiced when the infant holds his head up, rolls over, crawls, creeps, and finally stands up to free his hands, walks and moves through space to wield toys and tools, to play, learn, and create. These antigravity mechanisms are the "gyros" that must "match" with each other and function together for the establishment of a stable platform from which the child can launch his purposeful movements. They must provide consistent information for controlling with ease and precision the total movement of the child. The movement patterns acquired, through general body and body parts activities, build a body scheme. The child learns to throw, catch, run, hop, skip, walk the curb, somersault, stand on his head, cartwheel, etc. The body scheme thus acquired tells the child *where* he is. "A child sure of his balance knows where he is in space."[7] Emphasis must be placed on the need for the child to look, while he is exploring space and things and learning to move, so he may later know *where* he is by looking alone, without moving. Otherwise the patterns of movement and those of vision do not relate and vision will not adequately tell him *where* he is in relation to his environment.

The *second* area of performance observed is concerned with localized orientation, knowing where things are in relation to where the child is and where he knows himself to be. This is accomplished by movement of body parts with kinesthetic, tactual, and *visual* appraisals of the relationships found between self and surroundings. Again there is the need for emphasis for the child to be looking at, aligning eyes on, the thing moved or touched for the purposes of (1) steering and directing the movements and (2) matching the inputs of vision with inputs of the movement patterns.

The role of development is to bring the paired halves of the human into effective balance, with controlled thrusts and counter-thrusts. The importance of the interweaving of the two sides of the body, the two legs, two arms, two hands, two ears, and two *eyes* cannot be overstressed.[8] This bilaterality permits an effectualness of movement and manipulation, of reciprocal interweaving between parts and sides that leads to directionality of movement and the visual interpretation of directionality essential to knowing, and knowing the differences between, up, down, right, left, away, and toward. As the child explores the direction and extent of his movements, visually monitored, he learns to make some of the visual judgments that are contributors to his visuomotor perceptions. Bilaterality develops binocularity, *i.e.*, the effective matching of the inputs of the two eyes and the resulting efficient matching with prior experiences, stored in the cortex. Movement patterns to be encouraged are those of patting, pulling, poking, pushing, cutting, pasting, coloring, drawing, kicking, tossing, batting, skating, dancing, etc.

Me-it relationships, which come from movement in and through space, provide the child the opportunity to integrate his body scheme data with visual information and gain the orientation of self with his environment.[9] He can know *where he is* and *where it is* and is ready for knowing *what it is.*

The *third* area of performance provides identification or *whatness* to the objects in the environment of the child. The manipulation of things—by such movements as feeling, rubbing, mouthing, tasting, throwing, hefting, listening, smelling, and looking—develops sensitivities to textures, temperatures, tastes, weights, sounds, odors, sizes, shapes, distances, etc. Likenesses and differences emerge as patterns are matched, and as mismatches occur, as inputs are matched with previous experiences, and as sensory inputs are matched with each other. That is, things first are explored with direct contact, then as they are looked at and felt they begin to look like they feel, then feel like they look, and finally need only be looked at, without touching, and the child can "know" what it feels like, *what* it is, without further exploration of hand or mouth or nose or ear.

Knowing what a thing is, visually, is the result of matching the patterns of sight with the patterns of the other inputs (touch, taste, smell, hearing, and muscle movement) while the object is being explored. Then, with the trigger of light alone, from the object, the child can identify, know the object; know what it would feel like if he touched it, without touching it; know what it would smell like, without smelling it, etc.

At this stage he can begin to decide what the object means to him, what it can do for him, how it will help or harm him, whether to choose or reject it, ignore or select it for value or pleasure. If the matches have been adequately made, he can make the judgments on visual patterns alone. If not, he will be observed reverting to earlier stages of recontacting the object for clarification, confirmation, verification, and reinforcement. As he perfects the matches and increases the storage of information, his movements become more and more effective, more economic, less random and more purposeful, more controlled. The mobility leads to immobility, reduces the need to move in order to know. The only movements needed to know are, at this stage, the movements of eyes. Vision is beginning to be what it will finally be, the dominant process of development and learning.

The *fourth* area of performance is one of communication, of language or speech and audition. Early sounds made by the infant are repetitive, practicing to explore and perfect the range, volume, tone, and expression. His imitative sounds lead to imitative speech, discovery of likenesses and differences in speech sounds, and the beginning of matching his patterns of speech sounds with objects, events, sequences, and experiences acquired through movement. Matches are made between the speech sounds he hears others say and those he says and thus he learns to speak the mother tongue. As he talks to himself and his pretend friends he learns the skill of communicating his experiences to others, his movements and contacts with his world. He learns he can reduce movement, time, and effort by using language to exchange information, experiences, ideas, opinions, likes, dislikes, and needs. When he lacks appropriate words he falls back on movement to demonstrate, show, or pantomime what he needs to say. These very movements bring about new orientational skills, frames of reference, and new meanings to old words, and prepare understandings and meanings for new words.[10]

The child needs to be encouraged to listen and differentiate speech sounds to perfect his own audition and in turn his own speech. He needs to talk about things he does as he does them and looks at them, thus expanding the match between all the patterns of inputs— sight, sound, speech, movement, touch, etc. By so doing, the foundation is laid for the high visual component of language—the ability to visualize the thing, place, person, event, sequence, relationships, and moods triggered by a word or words heard or said. When, at a later time, a symbol, a picture, or a printed or written word is seen, the child can name the symbol and from the patterns of speech and audition conjure up all the related matched stored movement patterns and 'know" the full meaning for which the symbol stands. When finally he can drop out saying and listening to the word, he need only look at the word and know. This is one of our goals for the child in our culture—to be skilled in rapidly, meaningfully, and silently interpreting symbols of the mother tongue.

These four areas of performance are not isolated and unrelated but overlap each other in time, movement, space, emphasis, and needs as development progresses. There is constant interplay among them as they interact and produce a unity of behavior. Each influences and modifies the others. Their collective and separate sequence of development is cyclical, almost never-ending, and sequential only to the extent that the sequences are limited by the growth and maturation of the structures that move and control the moving. That is, speech and listening, for example, are not last to develop because they were named last in our discussion. They need not be, indeed are not, delayed until the child knows *where he is*, can walk and know *where things are*. The first cry and the "goo" of the infant are speech in the making and come before he has learned to cope with gravity or learned to move eyes accurately to follow hand.

The overlapping of the four areas of performance can be thought of, in this model of vision development and learning, as an emergent that is known as *vision*. Vision is the combining and efficient utilization of these four processes and stages. Vision is the derivative of all the underlying processes and modes of performance. Vision must become dominant, replacing and substituting for, in the order of development, all the other sensory and motor systems. Only then can vision be the process through which one does most of his learning, once the skill of reading has been acquired.

In summary, visual development demands that the child learn to move himself, by means of his own movement, learn how to participate as a sighted, visually steered, and visually directed, multisystemmed, controlled organism. As time and growth occur, previous stages of development are reexperienced by means of visualization— reviewed and remembered as if the original actions were actually repeated—or the original auditory judgments, visual judgments, or tactual judgments—and all are related through the ability to visualize for comparisons and analysis. Finally, finding there are pictures, words, or numbers that express these experiences and visualizations, he can read, communicate with himself and others through symbols, and eliminate all hindrances of time and space.

Thus he can learn and hopefully earn in our culture within the demands of our society utilizing this supreme process of vision.

HOMER HENDRICKSON, O.D.

REFERENCES

[1] G.N. Getman, *How to Develop Your Child's Intelligence* (Luverne, Minn., Announcer Press, 1957).

[2] Maria Montessori, *The Discovery of the Child* (Madras, India, Kalakshetra Publications and Wheaton, Ill., The Theosophical Press, 1948).

[3] C. Judson Herrick, *The Evolution of Human Nature* (Austin, University of Texas, 1956).

[4] Richard S. Fixott, *American Journal of Opthalmology*, August, 1957.

[5] A.M. Skeffington, Courses and Lectures presented by the Optometric Extension Program, Duncan, Oklahoma, 1928–1967.

[6] Arnold Gesell, F. Ilg, G.E. Bullis, G.N. Getman, and V. Ilg, *Vision, Its Development in Infant and Child.* (New York, Paul Hoeber, 1949).

[7] Bonnie Prudden, *Is Your Child Really Fit?* (New York, Harper & Bros., 1956).

[8] G.N. Getman, "The Role of the Visuomotor Complex in the Acquisition of Learning Skills," *Childhood Aphasia and Brain Damage*, vol. III. Norristown, Pa., The Pathway School, 1966.

[9] G.N. Getman, "The Four L's of Learning." (Van Nuys, Calif., Media, 1967).

[10] G.N. Getman, *Development of Vision* (Duncan, Okla., Optometric Extension Program, 1950–51, 1957–61).

Samuel Kirk and G. Orville Johnson speak of Montessori's contributions to the education of both the mentally defective and the preschool normal child in their Educating the Retarded Child:

"Auto-education," or self-teaching, was the keynote of the Montessori system. Activities and material were so organized and designed that the children taught themselves while the teacher withdrew into the background, merely supervising the activities. This self-teaching method was carried out by means of didactic materials.

As Carl Byoir has noted in the National Education Association Addresses and Proceedings, *Montessori found in the methods of physiological sense training a formula that she later applied with the method of the experimental psychologist to the education of normal children. "With a splendid knowledge of the history of methods,"* he says, *"Dr. Montessori has combined the fruits of special training: as a physician, she learned the physical needs of the child: as a teacher of deficient children, she mastered the methods of sense training; to an exact knowledge of psychology and anthropology she added an inventive mechanical genius probably unrivaled in the history of education."*

CURRICULAR CONSIDERATIONS IN PROGRAMS FOR THE RETARDED: APPLICATION OF THE MONTESSORI MODEL

Maria Montessori, M.D., was first a physician, then an educator; she also managed to be a thorough student of philosophy, psychology, and anthropology. She became known for her lifetime endeavors on behalf of the child, developing a system of education that included programmed preparation for learning, unique methods, and the only systematic collection of educational devices designed first for retarded children and modified later for use by normal children. In an era when education was stereotyped and discipline in the schools was almost brutal, an era that exploited child labor and placed retarded children in insane asylums, she fought for early childhood education and education of the retarded, while proposing revolutionary changes in curriculum and methods.

Montessori's theoretical writings contain many rhetorical generalizations from which it is difficult to construct a model, or "road map," yet her notes on techniques for using her teaching or didactic material are more detailed and precise than any other available today. Montessori based her assumptions or hypotheses concerning how the child develops and matures as a learning creature upon her observations of the child's behavioral responses to the materials she presented to him. She stated in her classic work, *The Montessori Method*: "The method used by me is that of making a pedagogical experiment with a didactic object and awaiting the spontaneous reaction of the child."[1] She thus experimentally went through a set of inductive operations and derived certain conclusions from her observations. It should be noted, however, that in her development of a method for educating normal children, she began with assumptions derived from her experiences in teaching retarded children. Her original "road map" had to be modified to fit the new terrain and she left us only a few clues as to the specific changes that were made.

Guided by the works of Itard and Seguin, two pioneers in special education, Montessori designed and had manufactured a large variety of didactic material. She states, however, that "unless these materials were rightly presented they failed to attract the attention of the deficients." Both Seguin and Montessori believed that the basis of all work with the mentally deficient was primarily spiritual; *i.e.*, the love, respect, understanding, and patience of the teacher must awaken the spirit of the child. The moral preparation of the teacher for this work was considered the key to successful teaching of the retarded by Seguin and Montessori. Both stressed that mechanical teaching, whereby the teacher followed the rules to the letter in using the didactic apparatus, was rarely successful. It is still true today that materials and techniques are useless unless the teacher understands the reasons for their use and can also awaken the child's interest in working with them. Our literature is full of words like "motivation," "drive," "stimulus," and "response"; we rarely mention words or concepts such as "love," "compassion," "spirit," or "faith." Yet, without these qualities how can the teacher hope to teach the child, especially the subnormal? When these qualities are absent, how can she awaken the interest of the child?

Montessori's method is largely based on the concept described by Seguin: "To lead the child, as it were, by the hand, from the education of the muscular system, to that of the nervous system, and of the senses," and then "from the education of the senses to general notions, from general notions to abstract thought, from abstract thought to morality."[2] Upon this also she built her own methods for teaching mathematics and language: speaking, reading, and writing.

In *Dr. Montessori's Own Handbook*, she outlined her three-part method: "The technique of my method as it follows the natural physiological and psychological development of the child, may be divided into three parts: (1) Motor education; (2) Sensory education; and (3) Language, or intellectual education. The care and management of the environment itself afford the principal means of motor education, while sensory education and education of language are provided for by my didactic material."[3]

Elsewhere, she stated: "If it were necessary to compress the description of the Montessori method into a single phrase, perhaps the most comprehensive would be that it was a method based on 'Liberty in a Prepared Environment.' "[4] Montessori discussed such specific limits of liberty as the limits of interest, ability, knowledge, and "the collective interest of the community in which the child functions." Within the "prepared environment," she provided objects designed through their use to achieve some definite purpose, to allow the child to carry out a real piece of work having a practical objective. "To spread the table cloth for the actual setting of the table at the dinner hour and to fold it up and replace it accurately when the meal is over; to wash up the dishes and replace every item in its own place in the cupboard—these are pieces of work which are graduated not only as regards successive difficulties of execution, but which demand a gradual development of character, because of the patience which is necessary for carrying them out and the responsibility which they involve in order that they should be carried into effect."[5] These activities are called *exercises in practical life.*

The prepared environment includes the opportunity for movement and motor training, movable, child-sized equipment and furniture, and—of major importance—the provisions for order. The child is to be guided from the start by presenting him with activities that he is prepared to do and at which he can be successful.

The concept of order in Montessori is particularly applicable to the education of the retarded child. Each activity is made up of a graded series of movements to be performed in logical sequence. Montessori broke down each exercise of practical life into "points of interest," specific points within each exercise to which the child's attention is drawn, thus leading to a detailed acquisition of movements or steps within each exercise. As the child is taught each "exercise," such as washing hands, polishing shoes, or cutting vegetables, each step of the operation is presented by the teacher verbally and by demonstration in logical, orderly sequence, very much as though she were programming a computer. The child is being trained to focus his attention and to analyze his body movements as he repeats the sequence each time. He is also learning to develop efficient motor patterns and orderly movement. As the child's attention is directed to proprioceptive and external cues, essentially he is being trained to use feedback from his own action and from the external situation. This approach is of value in working with trainable children, who require precise and careful direction.

Motor education includes the exercises of practical life and gymnastics such as: "the primary movements of everyday life (walking, rising, sitting, handling objects); the care of the person; management of the household; gardening; manual work; gymnastic exercises; and rhythmic movements."[6] She designed materials for learning to dress and undress, such as buttoning, tying, hooking, and lacing frames. Children are taught to wash, set the table, polish shoes, sweep and mop the floor, pour juices and milk, serve food, clean up after eating, etc. In each of these activities, she said, the teacher must at the beginning teach the child with few or no words at all, but with very precise actions.

Gardening and manual activity are considered important means of gaining the child's interest, and she pointed out that agriculture was applied with some success on a large scale in the education of the mentally deficient in Paris. For manual instruction she provided clay work, teaching the children to construct useful tiles, vases, and even bricks. With the latter, children may make patios, walls, and even small playhouses.

The exercise of "walking the line" is useful in gymnastic work. The children learn to walk heel-to-toe along a line about two inches wide, like tight-rope walkers. There are innumerable variations of this exercise, all directed toward the development of balance and coordination. Rope ladders, suggested by Seguin, are recommended to help the child develop general strength, prehension, and co-ordination. (Seguin also recommended the trampoline.) Music is added to many of the exercises, such as "walking the line," and the children gradually tend to develop a sense of rhythm.

The Montessori materials used for sensory education represent a selection from material used by Itard and Seguin, from objects used as tests in experimental psychology, and from material designed by Montessori herself. These materials are fairly familiar to most of us today, especially since the resurgence of interest in Montessori. However, much of the material she used for the retarded was abandoned in the education of the normal child, while much that she retained she had to modify. Let us consider, for example, the cylinder inserts. These are three blocks of wood, in each of which is inserted a row of ten small cylinders. In one series, the row of cylinder inserts are all of the same height but have diameters that decrease from thick to thin. In the second, the inserts all have the same diameter but decrease in height. In the third, the cylinder inserts decrease in both height and diameter. In a classroom of *normal* preschool children, this is an exercise presented to three-year-olds and is often one of the favorites. However, she pointed out that it would be necessary to begin the *retarded* child with simpler exercises in which the stimuli were much more strongly contrasted, and many other exercises would have to precede work with the cylinder blocks.

Montessori stated that once she was able to present the cylinder blocks to the retarded child it was necessary to continually recall his attention. When he succeeded in correctly placing one of the inserts he lost interest and stopped the game. When he committed an error, it was necessary for the teacher to correct it or to urge him to correct it himself; when he was able to correct an error he tended to be indifferent. She wrote "The difference in reaction between deficient and normal children, in the presentation of didactic material made up of graded stimuli, is plainly seen from the fact that *the same didactic material used with deficients makes education possible, while with normal children it provokes autoeducation.*"

Montessori provided much material for sensorimotor training. The didactic materials are designed to attract the child's attention, to "educate the senses," and to allow manipulation by the child. The goal is to assist the child in his task of creating order and sequence in sensory input by presenting a carefully constructed sequence of experience that proceeds very slowly from the concrete to the abstract. These materials are grouped according to sense: auditory, visual, tactile, baric (weight), gustatory, olfactory, and stereognostic. They are subgrouped according to specific qualities such as sound intensity, pitch, form, dimension, color, texture, weight, taste, and odor. Each sense is trained in isolation. Contrasts are always presented to the child first, then identities are established through matching, and finally, gradations of quality are presented for finer discrimination.

The idea of always presenting two contrasting stimuli rather than a single one was derived from Seguin. He also developed the "three-period lesson" to associate an object or a quality with its name. Both Seguin and Montessori stressed the necessity of using the "three-period lesson" in teaching the retarded child.

The first period consists of establishing identity, *associating* the sense perception with its name. The teacher presents, for instance, the longest and the shortest rod and says, "This is short. This is long." For the retarded child she may repeat this many times, slowly and clearly. No other words are used, in order to avoid confusing the child.

The second period tests the child's *recognition* of the object corresponding to the name. After the name has been presented by the teacher for a suitable period of time, she may ask, "Which is short?" or "Which is long?" If the child points correctly, the rods are mixed and the teacher repeats the questions, continuing to strengthen and fix the association until the child is ready for some other activity.

The third period is verification that the child can *recall* the name corresponding to the object. Now the child is simply asked, upon being shown, say, the short rod: "What is this?" The teacher may now work on correct articulation, and considerable repetition is usually required.

The "three-period lesson" may be slow and tedious, but it is effective. The period of time between success in the second and in the third periods (*i.e.*, between recognition and recall) is often quite lengthy and provides a striking illustration of the amount of time and repetition required for a child to establish the associations so necessary in language development. Vocabulary, wherever and however you find it, has to be committed to memory, one way or another.

Part of the sensory education includes many exercises performed by the child in blindfold. The normal child loves to exercise his skill at identifying textures, sounds, smells, shapes, etc., while blindfolded. However, the retarded child may go to sleep in darkness, or he may focus his attention on the blindfold itself, thereby losing the purpose of the exercise. Thus, not all of the techniques observed in a Montessori class for normal preschool children can be applied to the retarded child.

Nonetheless, the basic principles in sensory education do apply as well to the retarded child: One should proceed from few stimuli, strongly contrasting, to many stimuli in gradual differentiation always more fine and imperceptible; sensory education should precede naming the objects; the association of the sense perception with its name should be presented through the "three-period lesson."

It is in the teaching of writing and reading that Montessori departs from Seguin and Itard. Seguin attempted to teach retarded children to write by first teaching them design, and his was a most tedious and arduous method both for the teacher and the pupil. Montessori first came upon her ideas for teaching writing when she tried unsuccessfully to teach a retarded eleven-year-old girl to darn with needle and thread. She switched to weaving with the Froebel mats, a form of darning but with strips of paper that are threaded through others. After the girl became skilled in the Froebel paper weaving, she was able to take up darning with success. As a result of this observation, Montessori developed techniques for preparing the child's hand. She stated, "I saw that preparatory movements could be carried on, and reduced to a mechanism, by means of repeated exercises not in the work itself but in that which prepares for it." This recalls J. McV. Hunt's statement that "The experiential roots of a given schema lie in antecedent activities different in structure from the schema to be observed and measured."[8]

To prepare the hand for writing, Montessori provided various exercises that require the child to use his thumb, index and middle fingers for grasping—for example, the touch boards, the various pouring exercises, and more directly, the coloring in of the metal insets, and the sandpaper letters, all providing tactile and kinesthetic exercises. She found that although some of her retarded children had become proficient in tracing the sandpaper letters, the children had to be trained to hold a pencil, which requires a special muscular mechanism. In her first book, she gave a detailed description of how she taught the retarded children to write and to read, summarizing, "Touching the letters and looking at them at the same time, fixes the image more quickly through the cooperation of the senses. Later, the two facts separate; looking becomes reading; touching becomes writing. According to the type of individual, some learn to read first, others to write."[9] She pointed out also that mechanical reading, reading without comprehension, precedes true reading, or the interpretation of an idea from the graphic symbols.

Montessori taught her retarded children to read and to write. Whether these were children we would today call educable or trainable, or both, we cannot know. Her method is so clearly and precisely described, however, that we could well test it. The three basic steps in teaching the child to write are: (1) preparation of the muscular mechanism for holding and using the pencil; (2) use of the sandpaper letter to establish the visual-motor image of the graphic symbols and to establish the kinesthetic memory of the movements necessary to writing, associating these with the sounds of the letters; and (3) use of the movable alphabet to compose words that are first "sounded out" by the child. Mechanical reading is a natural progression from word building, and eventually to true interpretive reading.

In conclusion, Montessori wrote in her *Handbook*: "The functions to be established by the child fall into two groups: (1) The motor functions by which he is to secure his balance and learn to walk and to coordinate his movements; (2) the sensory functions through which, receiving sensations from his environment, he lays the foundations of his intelligence by a continued exercise of observation, comparison and judgment. In this way he gradually comes to be acquainted with his environment and to develop his intelligence."[10]

She provided an environment prepared, both physically and psychologically, for the child. She demanded humility and careful clinical observation on the part of the teacher. Her method and materials were designed to allow programmed preparation for learning and systematic motor and sensory education. ⟳

In the words of J. McV. Hunt, in his Introduction to *The Montessori Method*: "Montessori has provided a model. According to the impressionistic reports of observers, her 'Houses of Children' worked quite well. We can well emulate Montessori's model, but we should not stop with it. Moreover, in the future those who become concerned with the question of the effectiveness of Montessori's model, and of revisions to come, should have more than the impressionistic reports of observers to go on. They should have demonstrations employing the experimental method and the best techniques available for educational and psychological assessment."[11]

SYLVIA ONESTI RICHARDSON, M.D.

REFERENCES

[1] Maria Montessori, *The Montessori Method* (New York, Stokes, 1912), p. 167.

[2] Edouard Seguin, *Idiocy and Its Treatment by the Physiological Method* (New York, 1866).

[3] R.C. Orem, ed., *A Montessori Handbook* (New York, Putnam's, 1965), p. 47.

[4] Maria Montessori, *The Child in the Church* (London, Sands, 1929), p. 110.

[5] ———, *The Montessori Method.*

[6] R.C. Orem, ed., *A Montessori Handbook*, p. 66.

[7] Maria Montessori, *The Montessori Method*, p. 169.

[8] J. McV. Hunt, "The Psychological Basis for Using Preschool Enrichment as an Antidote for Cultural Deprivation." Speech given at Arden House Conference on Preschool Enrichment, Dec., 1962.

[9] Maria Montessori, *The Montessori Method*, p. 266.

[10] R.C. Orem, ed., *A Montessori Handbook*, p. 169.

[11] J. McV. Hunt, "Introduction," *The Montessori Method*, by Maria Montessori (New York, Schocken, 1964), p. XXXV.

In The Case for Early Reading, *the editor, with George Stevens, has assembled the historical and contemporary evidence from many disciplines indicating that children can and* should *learn to read in the preschool period. The most significant study of the effectiveness of teaching reading in kindergarten to date has been done by Paul McKee and Joseph Brzeinski in the Denver Public Schools. It involved approximately 4,000 pupils and extended from kindergarten through fifth grade. The kindergarten beginning reading instruction demonstrated a measurable, positive continuing effect.* No evidence was found that this instruction in beginning reading affected visual acuity, created problems of school adjustment, or caused dislike for reading.*

That most children are not taught to read earlier is attributed by these researchers to two factors: the tradition of reading readiness and unjustified fear of harmful results. They conclude by suggesting that we consider the possibility of introducing in addition to reading, other language, writing, science, and number skills to the preschool child.

The editor would also suggest that we experiment with the systematic exposure of preschoolers to the various art forms, and organize the environment to encourage creative expression. Shinichi Suzuki likes to begin teaching Japanese children to play the violin when they are three. By the time the students of this revolutionary teacher are seven, many are playing concertos by Vivaldi and Bach.

MONTESSORI AND MATHEMATICAL ILLITERACY

A recent extensive international study of mathematics teaching and learning, as reported by Fred M. Hechinger in the New York *Times*, ranked the United States quite low on the International Testing Scale, considerably behind many other countries with comprehensive systems, and far beneath the impressive scores of the first-ranking country, Japan.

True, the "new math" is being rapidly introduced to our students, but without thorough retraining of teachers, the new math may not

---

* The gains from the experimental program were evident in both reading comprehension and reading vocabulary.

produce the results that it should. New techniques will be filtered through people committed to old methods. And without a change in the attitudes of children in the public schools, the new math may fail, no matter how well presented. A child who is conditioned in his preschool years to believe that numbers are both difficult and boring will have a difficult time when faced in first grade with paper, pencil, and the need for correct calculations.

Of course, mathematical illiteracy is not new, but the new imperative of mathematical competency in our technological society demands that we no longer be complacent about such illiteracy. In this regard, there is a great deal to be learned from the work of Maria Montessori, who developed special materials and techniques to introduce the nursery-age child to mathematics and to enhance his interest, success, and confidence in mathematics throughout his life.

She believed that the educated person should be fluent with a variety of symbol systems: verbal language, a musical score, statistical material, for example.

Our civilization is based upon mathematics. Architecture, communications, navigation, aeronautics—all science and technology—depend upon mathematical calculations. Today, most of our legislation is based on statistics, and it is impossible to decide the questions of politics in an intelligent way without some knowledge of mathematics. The human mind itself is being studied mathematically, and such tools as intelligence quotients are helping interpret the workings of the mind. Health and safety progress is based on the interpretation of statistical information. The history of mathematics shows that since the time of the Sumerians it has been natural for man to count and measure. This capacity for exactness in observation, which corresponds to a regularity in natural phenomena, led to the discovery of natural laws and to the development of knowledge to control our environment. If this study of mathematics is begun early enough, the student will be as much "at home" with numbers as he is with words. Mathematics history indicates that numbers and youth go together—that many great mathematical discoveries have been made before college entrance age, and a decline in mathematical achievement may set in after the age of twenty-five.

Gauss, the German "prince of mathematics," was able to do the four basic mathematical operations in his preschool years. When he was about three, looking over the shoulder of his father, who was doing the payroll for his construction workers, he discovered an error in addition that his father had made.

Study of mathematics can be a fascinating occupation for the very young child. So many parents develop a positive distaste for any work with numbers, because of the inadequate, rote method of learning that was, and often still is, common in the schools, that they are not able to give their young children a taste of the joys of mathematics. Instead, these parents project an image of dullness and ultimate failure that discourages mathematical literacy. They may be incapable of introducing even simple number operations to their children, for whom numbers remain mysterious or incomprehensible.

While there is currently great interest in language development, and often considerable concern for early reading, there is much less understanding of the possibilities of early mathematics, although mathematics may in fact be easier for the young child to grasp than reading.

As we realize the crucial importance of the mother's influence on the young child, we must find ways to involve the mother in the joy of numbers and to make her understand that, even if her own experiences were negative, great changes in the teaching of mathematics can make her child's chances for success much greater—if he does not come to school with expectation of failure already developed.

Parental interest in the "new math" is evidenced by the number of manuals designed specifically for parents, but even such advanced material is not necessary, especially if it creates tension on the part of parents who feel they must keep up with their children's mathematics but who cannot overcome the effects of their own bad schooling. What *is* necessary on the part of mothers is a serious attempt to separate their own emotions, carried over from repeated childhood failures, from their children's work, so that these mothers may give positive emotional support to the earliest efforts their children make to master number concepts.

In a Montessori school, young children can master reading, writing, and arithmetic. They do this without any difficulty because the subject matter is presented sensorily and absorbed gradually through the tactile and other senses. In this way, the child of pre-school age amasses knowledge "naturally" and easily. Montessori showed that it is not only possible but preeminently practical to introduce to preschoolers mathematical material traditionally considered suitable only for more advanced students.

Children in a Montessori class spend a great part of their time working on arithmetic and geometry. There are no external rewards for success or censure for failure. Children do this work because they are interested in it, tending to confirm the theory suggested by the great mathematician Pascal that the human intelligence is naturally mathematical. Montessori, herself, spoke at great length of the "mathematical mind" of the child. If the intelligence is permitted to develop naturally, she said, it will turn to counting and measuring. Montessori children first concentrate on exact work with three-dimensional concrete materials. Then they acquire a concept of numbers. From this they proceed to counting in the decimal system. The didactic material developed by Montessori provides excellent preparation for mathematics, and provides "materialized abstractions" leading to the understanding of numbers. The conventional method of teaching mathematics by pencil and paper, blackboard and chalk, is not used in the beginning stages of Montessori mathematics. Pencil and paper are very useful and convenient in appropriate circumstances, but a young child is not ready to plunge into abstract calculations.

Modern teaching of mathematics recognizes the importance of manipulating beads, blocks, and other concrete materials especially prepared for mathematical calculations. Montessori said it is necessary that children have a great deal of time to spend working with such mathematical apparatus. It is not enough that children be taught each operation in turn; it is not enough that they understand them. Understanding is only the beginning, a point of departure. The children must repeat these exercises with materialized abstractions until the knowledge becomes second nature—or, as Montessori put it, "absorbed by the unconscious."

The calculations of area and volume, of square, and square root are examples of instances in which algebra, arithmetic, and geometry are all involved. These operations may at first glance seem difficult for the "preschooler," but he applies himself eagerly to the tasks when they are presented in the form of concrete material. For children who use the Montessori material, arithmetic and geometry have never been arbitrarily separated as they are in traditional education. The Montessori golden beads give the young child a clear concept of the unit being a point, the ten a line, a hundred being a square—the square of ten—and the thousand being a cube—the cube of ten. Through manipulation of the Montessori mathematical apparatus, the child makes many discoveries—as did the people of ancient times, who worked with pebbles and sticks in making their first calculations.

Geometry as a subject concerned with the measurement and comparison of different shapes and sizes is particularly suitable for presentation in a concrete way. In a Montessori class, children have the opportunity to manipulate geometric solids and geometric inserts (which are used, too, for indirect preparation for writing). They are also given constructive triangles so the child learns to recognize shapes and to name them, thus acquiring an important element of geometry. In our present educational system, we often wait to present geometry until the child is eleven or twelve. By this time, however, he may have lost interest in shapes that belong to the sensorial period.

The Greek mathematicians, who were essentially geometrists, spent considerable time working with different shapes. They liked to play with dots, to arrange them in various ways, such as triangles, squares, and pentagons, and to study these formations. Young children in a Montessori class like to arrange chips (similar to poker chips) in various geometrical organizations. The young child has a great interest in shapes and forms because he has only recently started his exploration of space, which helps orient him to his environment. The concrete material gives him an opportunity to "program" some of this knowledge in his subconscious, to be brought out later during his study of geometry.

To illustrate some examples of the many mathematics possibilities built into the Montessori self-teaching material, let us consider but one piece of apparatus—the number rods.

The number rods are a series of ten wooden sticks of the same thickness (square cross section) but differing in length—the second one being twice as long as the first, the third three times as long as the first, and so on, the tenth being ten times as long. Montessori designed these rods in the metric system—the first rod is 1 dm × 2 cm × 2 cm, the tenth, 1 m × 2 cm × 2 cm. The rods are marked off into units, alternately colored red and blue. Rod one is red, two is red and blue, three is red-blue-red, and so on. They are fundamental units of material carefully designed for developing number concepts.

The children use the rods for various manipulations: counting them, comparing them, putting two of them together and finding them equal in length to a third rod or to another pair; forming them into "steps" by putting them side by side, or into a long line by putting them end to end for serial counting. When the rods have become familiar to the children, they can easily be linked with the number symbols by placing cards with the numbers printed on them next to the proper rods. Concepts that the rods can teach inductively include:

1. Quantitative relationship (each rod in relation to the other).

2. Concept of position in space (by organizing the rods into steps or long rows).

3. Concepts involved in measuring (the two-rod is twice as long as the one-rod, and so on—the rods can be used as measuring sticks).

4. Concept of a number as an aggregate of ones (the child can verify this by counting with the aid of the colors).

5. Concept of number as a whole (the rod of four, for example, is a whole but can easily be broken down into ones by serial counting).

6. Concept of the number symbol (by placing the number symbol next to the equivalent rod).

7. Concept of number in sequence (serial counting of the rods, either up to ten, or if arranged in one long line, up to fifty-five).

8. Concept of fraction (the five-rod, for example, is half of the ten-rod).

9. Concept of addition (putting together two rods, comparing with a third—for example, three-rod and two-rod as long as five-rod; this has the additional value that the numbers of wholes are added

rather than the aggregates of ones—for instance, $3+2=5$ is not derived from $[1+1+1] + [1+1] = 5$).

10. Concept of subtraction (analogous to addition).

The rods have a distinct advantage over other material. At a time when big-muscle movement is still very important and sitting at a table quite unnatural, work with the rods on a mat or the floor fits the preschooler's needs. The relatively large dimensions of the rods make the step from unit to unit very marked, and therefore progression is clear.

While the rods are not as abstract as spoken or written numbers but are real things that the child can perceive and handle, they are not of the nature of concrete objects that occur ordinarily in the child's experience, such as toys or coins. The rods, therefore, form a bridge to the higher level of abstraction represented by the number symbol. Making this next step by use of printed cards obviates reading from the blackboard or writing, and brings the symbol down to a more concrete level by enabling the child to handle it by touching or placing the card, or by tracing the symbol with his fingers.

Thus, we see that the apparently "simple" number rods—but one item in the array of Montessori materials—are laden with pedagogical possibilities.

LENA L. GITTER

The Montessori approach is being used with an expanding variety of groups of handicapped children.

A.T. Corcoran, former principal of a center for backward and maladjusted children, has indicated that "work with the Montessori material was in almost every case beneficial in smaller or greater measure to the children who attended this Center, and all, without exception, came to realize that for them to learn and to achieve was not only possible but was also an exciting adventure in which they and the teacher took part." Sister M. Gonzaga, in an article on Montessori's discoveries and influence, notes that "from the Sion Hill Montessori School in Dublin to the Kennedy Clinic in Santa Monica, disturbed and maladjusted children have been helped by the Montessori teacher." Miss M.E. Stephenson of the Washington Montessori Institute has used Montessori material successfully with the deaf at St. Joseph's School for the Deaf.

Dr. K. Murphy, visiting physician to St. Ultan's Hospital, notes that the Montessori class in the unit for children suffering from primary tuberculosis is recognized by the doctors as a valuable asset in the treatment of their patients. The equipment interests and occupies the children, and reduces boredom and restlessness. The Montessori directress is of help to the doctor in assessing the character and temperament of the child. She can, for example, be helpful when it comes to the question of discharging the patient. She can provide clues as to whether or not the child is amenable to discipline and likely to rest when at home.

The Children's Convalescent Hospital of Washington, D.C., has had a very successful Montessori school program funded by the Eugene and Agnes E. Meyer Foundation. The Montessori school, staffed by a certified Montessori teacher and an aide, serves the toddler (age range from one to three years) and preschool (two-and-a-half to six years) ward groups. Ward placement depends upon the child's physical and emotional development as well as chronological age. Diagnoses found in the school population include: failure to thrive, battered child syndrome, asthma, retardation, and personality adjustment problems. The Montessori school program is able to provide the children with order and security, and the opportunity to explore and work in structured freedom. Gradually, the children reach out for new material, tasks, and responsibilities. The directress makes extensive recordings of her observations, and is able to contribute a great deal of information in the psychiatric conferences and in informal discussion with the psychology and therapy staff.

The D.C. Society for Crippled Children also conducts Montessori classes for children, a number of them with multiple handicaps. The editor observed that the wide range of Montessori materials enables each child to choose and work with a piece of material appropriate to his level of functioning at the moment.

THE MONTESSORI METHOD AND THE EDUCATION OF THE DEAF

With the increased attention being given to the educational theories and instructional methods of Maria Montessori by laymen, psychologists, and educators, it is only natural that those interested in the education of the deaf should look afresh at the ideas of the remarkable Italian doctor to determine what, if anything, there is in her pedagogy that would assist in the improvement of the education of the deaf.

Of course, any discussion of the applicability of the Montessori method to the education of the deaf must be prefaced with a reservation. Maria Montessori did not develop her method with the education of the deaf child as a primary consideration, and, therefore, her method cannot be expected to solve all the unique problems confronting the teacher of the deaf. There is an essential difference in language development between the children with whom Montessori worked in her "Children's Houses" and deaf children. The children in the Case dei Bambini had a mastery of their native language. On the other hand, it is this very accomplishment that the great majority of deaf students do not possess. Therefore, whatever virtues the Montessori method may possess, there is little reason to believe that the teacher of the deaf will find in it a ready solution to the chief challenge that confronts him. This challenge can be summarized this way: how may his students achieve a level of language development enabling them to communicate fully in their environment, including use of language to learn subject matter. The fact that the children with whom Montessori worked generally had aural-oral command of their native language means that any application of the Montessori method to the deaf child necessitates an adaptation of some of her methods within the context of the established format of deaf education.

Despite this limitation, there are many facets of the Montessori method that can enhance the learning of the deaf child and therefore deserve investigation. Numerous contemporary students of educational theory and practice have found in Montessori a broadly based understanding of the learning process in human nature that seems to meet the needs of both the child's psychological and intellectual growth. Recently, her insights have been discussed at some length.[1]

Certainly, with the important exception of language, the deaf child's general educational needs are closely akin to, if not identical with, those of the hearing child. In this regard, Hans Furth has argued from his research that the intelligence of the deaf when measured by other than language-biased instruments tends to be normal.[2] From this we might expect that those components of the Montessori method that enhance the intellectual development of the normal child would perform a similar function for the deaf child.

That the education of the deaf is not approaching a point of perfection, and might profit from new ideas, has been discussed by Herbert R. Kohl in his paper "Language and Education of the Deaf." Kohl writes:

> Many claims have been made for the success of education for the deaf, mostly by teachers of the deaf. Closer scrutiny, however, reveals a very dismal picture. According to U.S. Government statistics, of the 1,104 students of sixteen years or more who for one reason or another left deaf schools in 1961–2, the 501 graduates had a grade level range of 3.1 (grade three, one month) to 12.8 in school achievement with a mean of 4.7, indicating that in general the deaf population is between four and seven years retarded.[3]

This relatively low level of academic accomplishment should stimulate those interested in deaf education to look for new and improved methods of instruction.

In this regard, there is some prospect that aspects of the Montessori method might be particularly valuable to the deaf child's mental development. One of the cardinal principles of the Montessori method is the systematic stimulation of all sensory channels. She designed and utilized educational apparatus that would promote learning through all of the senses: touch, seeing, hearing, and even smell.[4]

There is a related aspect of Montessori's sensory education that makes it most appropriate for deaf education. This is the special emphasis she placed upon the visual and tactile-kinesthetic modalities. Even a brief examination of her educational apparatus will reveal its extensive utilization of these sensory channels—the two channels usually open to the deaf child. In fact, with the important exception of her phonic reading materials, virtually all of her instructional apparatus is designed to be employed with a minimum of oral directions.

There is not space here to review all the Montessori apparatus; but one example of Montessori's tactile-visual orientation is the manner in which mathematics instruction is based on the manipulation of concrete objects. There are beads, blocks, rods, counting sticks, sandpaper figures, number cards—all carefully designed to teach inductively the basic mathematical principles and operations. These attractive materials are presented in stages that involve manipulation and visual examination on the child's part. After a few initial directions, the child is able to feel and see his way into mathematical insights, with the teacher giving individual lessons as needed. Much of the time the child is free to work at his own pace with materials he has selected. This autoinstructional dimension of the Montessori apparatus provides an important advantage. The child can work with most of the learning devices for extended periods of time with a minimum of guidance. This independent quality of the Montessori teaching apparatus results from its programmed character. Long before the current vogue in teaching machines and programmed instruction, Montessori had designed and developed materials in which the learning increments were small enough to be manageable and provide sequential successes. Error was controlled by immediate feedback to correct the learner's responses.

For example, one exercise involves fitting a set of wooden cylinders into matching holes. If there is an error in placing the cylinders into the appropriate holes, one cylinder will remain that does not fit into the opening that is left, and the child will go back over the series to correct his own error of size estimate. The teacher is only rarely required.

This example serves to illustrate a principle that prevails throughout the Montessori method: autoinstruction through the self-correction of error. The result of the application of this principle is that children can work individually. This system also accomplishes another important objective; it frees the teacher to assist individual learners who may be encountering special difficulties.

An ancillary aspect of Montessori's autoinstructional devices is the opportunity for "discovery" in learning. Montessori believed with John Dewey that we learn best by "doing" and she shared his distrust of education that depends exclusively upon the mastery and reproduction of spoken or written materials. Again, like Dewey, she believed that the best learning takes place when the learner makes active responses to problems rather than relatively passive responses to a lecture.

For Montessori, real learning involves a situation in which changes take place within the learner, and education must be student-centered in the sense that the student must be active in the learning process. Traditional educational practices, as recent learning theorists have pointed out, tend to be teacher-centered. With the Montessori method, as with modern programmed materials, the student is actively engaged in making responses to graded problems and the teacher functions as a monitor in the process. The teacher or "directress," in the Montessori terminology, intervenes only when the child is blocked at some point and unable to proceed unaided.

These educational principles led Montessori to develop methods that provide the student with an opportunity to learn by seeing and manipulating as well as by reading and listening. The fact that Montessori's didactic apparatus favors the visual and the tactile-kinesthetic modes of learning should be of special value to the educator of the deaf.

Another area of Montessori's educational theories may have special value for those interested in improving the education of the deaf. This is Montessori's special emphasis on early education. She believed that, properly exposed to prepared educational experiences, the child could begin his intellectual development at the age of three. In the Montessori system, reading, writing, and arithmetic are introduced between three and six years rather than being postponed, as is conventionally done, until the first grade.

This early start has special implications for the deaf child who, according to studies, is retarded at least four to five years at the conclusion of his secondary education. It is possible that the Montessori method, with its stress on early learning, can capitalize on the period of time in which the deaf child suffers his greatest intellectual deprivation—his early childhood. For it is during the critical preschool period that the deaf child falls behind his hearing contemporary. This is particularly true in the area of language development. The normal child brings to the first grade a vocabulary of as many as ten thousand spoken words while the deaf child has often barely begun his language development.

As time passes, this lag between the hearing and the deaf child continues or even increases, and to all intents and purposes the deaf child never catches up. The answer, in part at least, would seem to be a program of nursery school and kindergarten to provide the deaf child with an earlier start in all aspects of his intellectual development.

The pedagogy developed by Montessori stresses the importance of the formative years from birth to six for the mental growth of children. She believed that experiences during this critical period can stimulate or limit the child's intellectual potential. Whatever potential a child may inherit, its development depends on environmental stimulation for realization.

When the Italian doctor advanced this concept of early learning, many of her contemporaries disagreed. At the time, the prevailing school of thought in psychology favored the belief that traits were genetically determined and emerged automatically regardless of variations in environmental stimulation. However, the notion that a human characteristic such as intelligence is not greatly influenced by the environment has not fared well in the light of rapidly accumulating research, including important longitudinal studies.[5] Dr. J. McV. Hunt has dealt with the current view of environmental effects on the development of intelligence, while tracing the evolution of psychological thought on this subject dating from the turn of the century.[6]

Not only did Montessori hold that the child could learn early but—what is even more significant—that there were in the human nervous system critical periods during which the system could undergo its maximum rate of growth. Once these periods are past it becomes increasingly difficult to achieve maximum development. An excellent illustration of the importance of early stimulation in learning is the phenomenon of language acquisition. Under normal circumstances language is mastered by the child in the preschool period. When it is not so mastered, subsequent learning problems frequently result.[7]

Neurologist Wilder Penfield has traced language development in *Speech and Brain Mechanisms*.[8] One of his chief conclusions is that timing is of great importance in learning language. He describes as the "uncommitted cortex" those areas of the brain that must be stimulated in order to ensure intellectual development. Penfield points out that those who acquire two languages in childhood seem to be subsequently more adept in mastering new languages. Penfield's idea of the "uncommitted cortex" and Montessori's concept of "sensitive periods" represent two disciplines converging upon the same conclusion.

An important question to ask in relation to the critical or sensitive periods of learning involves what deprivation takes place when these periods are missed or passed by with little intellectual stimulation. There has been an attempt to estimate the magnitude of this deprivation by Dr. Benjamin S. Bloom of the University of Chicago. In his book *Stability and Change in Human Characteristics*, Dr. Bloom reviews the research assessing the growth of intelligence. Bloom has concluded that the environment will have its greatest effect on human development in areas such as intelligence during the period in which the characteristic is undergoing its greatest rate of change.

Among many human characteristics that follow this pattern, Bloom stresses particularly intelligence, which is largely stabilized by the age of eighteen. Bloom charts its rate of development until that age and finds that at least 20 percent of IQ potential is achieved by the age of one, 50 percent by about age four, 80 percent by age eight, and 90 percent by age thirteen.

This means that by the age of four, 50 percent of a child's potential IQ has been determined. Bloom writes that "we would expect the variations in the environment to have relatively little effect on the

IQ after age eight, but we would expect such variation to have marked effect on the IQ before that age, with the greatest effect likely to take between the ages of about one to five."[9]

This is precisely the period for which the Montessori method is designed. It would appear that she, working in the early years of this century, anticipated this most current educational principle. Indeed, as of this date, the full impact of Dr. Bloom's work, which appeared in 1965, has yet to be felt. Sixty years ago Dr. Montessori not only recognized the value of early education but designed a pedagogy that has introduced thousands of children all over the world to the advantages of early intellectual stimulation.

Considering the very special educational problems of the deaf, it would seem most appropriate for educators of the deaf to examine the ideas and devices of the Montessori method today.

GEORGE L. STEVENS

REFERENCES

[1] R.C. Orem, ed., *Montessori for the Disadvantaged* (New York, Putnam's, 1967).

[2] Hans G. Furth, "The Influence of Language on the Development of Concept Formation in Deaf Children," *Journal of Abnormal and Social Psychology*, Vol. 63 (1961), pp. 386–389.

[3] Herbert R. Kohl, "Language and Education of the Deaf." New York, Center for Urban Education, 1966, p. 4.

[4] R.C. Orem, *A Montessori Handbook* (New York, Putnam's, 1965), pp. 82–85.

[5] ———, "Preschool Patterning and Language Learning," *National Catholic Kindergarten Review*, Spring, 1966.

[6] J. McV. Hunt, *Intelligence and Experience* (New York, Ronald, 1961).

[7] G.L. Stevens and R.C. Orem, *The Case for Early Reading* (St. Louis, Mo., Warren H. Green, 1967).

[8] Wilder Penfield, and Lamar Roberts, *Speech and Brain Mechanisms* (Princeton, N.J., Princeton University Press, 1959).

[9] Benjamin Bloom, *Stability and Change in Human Characteristics* (New York, Wiley, 1965), p. 68.

SOME EARLY REFERENCES TO MONTESSORI AND SPECIAL CHILDREN

Since I have been preoccupied for years with the study of the child's psyche, I am in deep sympathy with your understanding and humanitarian endeavors, and my daughter, who is an analytical pedagogue, considers herself one of your disciples.*

BIBLIOGRAPHICAL REFERENCES

Anderson, Mrs. J. Scott, "The Montessori Method of Teaching Hearing Children." *Volta Review*, 14, June, 1912, pp. 154–168.

Bates, Laura, "Montessori Models." *American Annals of the Deaf*, 58, January, 1913, pp. 16–25.

Bell, Mrs. Alexander Graham, "What the Montessori Method Means to Me." *Freedom for the Child*, 1, 1914, pp. 7–10.

Hurd, Anna, "The Montessori Method Applied to Deaf Children." *Volta Review*, 17, June, 1915, pp. 239–242.

Long, J. Schuyler, "The Montessori Method: A Comparison." *American Annals of the Deaf*, 58, March, 1913, pp. 117–125.

Margulies, Reno, "Dr. Montessori and Her Method." *American Annals of the Deaf*, 58, September, 1913, pp. 496–502.

———, "Montessori Method Applicable to the Deaf." *Volta Review*, June, 1912, pp. 146–147.

"Montessori Method and the Subnatural Mind." Conference of Educational Associations (London), *Report of the 18th Annual Conference*, 1930, pp. 23–27.

Smith, Sadie, "The Montessori System and the Deficients." *Ohio Educational Monthly*, 62, August, 1913, pp. 431–434.

Weill, Blanche, "The Montessori Method and Sub-Normal Children." *The Call of Education*, 2, 1925, pp. 283–292.

---

* Sigmund Freud, in letter to Maria Montessori, 1917. Ernst L. Freud, ed., *The Letters of Sigmund Freud*. New York, McGraw-Hill, 1960, pp. 319–320.

MONTESSORI AND THE SLOW-LEARNING CHILD: PROMISE AND CHALLENGE

Who is the slow-learning child? The slow learner is frequently identified as a child whose intelligence quotient (IQ) is between 75 and 90. That is, he may have less capacity to gain from his experiences than do most children of his chronological age (CA), or his experiences may have been different. Intellectual development (mental age or MA) tends to level off at about sixteen years; that is, by sixteen, most people have learned the basic cognitive skills they will need to get along effectively, skills such as differentiation, abstraction, generalization, consideration of cause-and-effect sequences in inference and deduction, and fluency in dealing with verbal and mathematical relationships on a symbolic level. The child with an IQ of 75 may be expected, however, to "level off" with the mental skills typically acquired by twelve years of age. Such children are not usually retarded enough to be placed in special classes, yet they will have a difficult time keeping up with normal as well as bright children.

One challenge to the teacher is to provide worthwhile and successful experiences for these children within the usual classroom setting. If intellectual potential is distributed normally, approximately 12 to 15 percent of the school-age population may be in the slow-learner IQ range. It is about these 12 to 15 percent that I am writing, not about the higher percentage of children, particularly from low-income families, whose intellectual potential is likely to far outdistance their environmental opportunities for the intellectual development measured by intelligence tests. The possibilities offered by the Montessori method for these educationally disadvantaged, "pseudoretarded" children are discussed elsewhere.[1]

The slow-learning child is slower to develop but does not appear to develop in a different way. This means that two children of the same MA who differ in CA are likely to show similar basic learning

SOME CHARACTERISTICS OF THE SLOW-LEARNING CHILD IN THE CLASSROOM

	BEHAVIOR CHARACTERISTICS	
	HANDICAPS	ASSETS
Intellectual and physical	less physical stamina poor motor coordination forgets quickly poor ability to abstract difficulty understanding instructions—easily confused short interest and attention span lack of associative, categorizing ability confused by new problems and complicated tasks unable to work independently lacks "common sense" of class level socially as well as intellectually finds it difficult to keep up with class	sensorimotor responses and hand-eye coordination better than symbolic response system can learn faster from concrete experiences than from abstract can learn from manipulation of materials more than from the construction itself
Social-emotional	easily discouraged releases emotions physically uses aggression to gain attention feelings of rejection by parent and others lacks self-confidence	will imitate and follow others responds well to acceptance, praise, and attention may be socially well adjusted with others of his ability
AREAS FOR DEVELOPMENT Intellectual	develop flexible spoken language systems and basic vocabulary enlargement improve reading and writing abilities reduce tendency to give stereotyped answers increase ability to see likeness and difference (discrimination) increase ability to abstract, to use increasingly inclusive categories increase cognitive ability to generalize from experience increase ability to draw conclusions from concrete experiences: inductive and deductive reasoning		
Social-emotional	increase ability to set standards for self; for self-criticism increase ability to discriminate and verbalize the cause-effect contingencies in interpersonal situations increase ability for voluntary, self-directed activity increase self-confidence and self of value as part of the class develop ability to follow sequences of directions		

characteristics and similar psychomotor development on experimental tasks. The brighter of two children of the same CA but different MAs will, by this definition, show different learning characteristics and have superior psychomotor skills. One implication of these observations is the possibility of extrapolation from general developmental and learning theories to curriculum sequences and teaching methods for the slow-learning child.

Concerning social adjustment, the retarded child seems more likely to develop such compensatory reactions to emotional problems as aggression, lack of interest, or anxiety rather than personality disorders such as autism. The usual emotional stresses experienced by the normal person may be intensified for the slow-learning individual due to the restrictions his limited intellectual ability places on (a) his understanding of environmental cause-and-effect sequences, (b) the development of a variety of adjustment mechanisms, and (c) flexibility in choosing different ways of coping with subtly changed situations. A fundamental problem in educating the slow-learning child for an independent and satisfying life is thus said to center around the effectiveness of his social adjustment.

Some of the ways in which the slow-learning child has been reported[2] to differ from the normal child in the classroom (where the environmental situation is more motivationally and intellectually complex than in a structured experimental task) are shown in the table, which is organized in terms of four categories of behavior characteristics: (a) handicaps to classroom attainment; (b) possible classroom assets; (c) intellectual, and (d) adjustment behaviors that may provide directions for educational programs. It should be remembered that not all slow-learning children will show these characteristics and that children who are not slow learners may sometimes behave in similar ways. There is always a need for repeated and careful observation in describing the range of a child's behavior in many situations and for caution in inferring the processes underlying it.

In summary, the table indicates four major areas for educational intervention: (a) encouraging, particularly through concrete, sensorimotor (as contrasted to symbolic) systems, the development of discrimination, abstraction, categorization, generalization, and inference; (b) encouraging the development of language skills coordinated with the stage of development of these basic cognitive processes; (c) development of persistence as contrasted to distractibility, of self-direction, of respect for self and for others; (d) encouraging the application of the cognitive-perceptual skills to interpersonal situations.

This formulation suggests both the promise of Montessori techniques and the challenge to them offered by the slow-learning child. Certain aspects of the Montessori approach seem immediately congruent with the characteristics of the "slow learner" as outlined above. These are:

(a) The emphasis on the primacy of sensorimotor skills as contrasted to verbal skills in an orderly intellectual development.

(b) The focus on *manipulation* of materials and direct experience in the development of discrimination and generalization.

(c) The proceed-at-your-own-rate aspect in which the child develops as he is able rather than in relation to the pace of a group of other children.

(d) *The naturally mixed CA classrooms.*

(e) The utilization of imitation of older children by younger children, which would come easily to slow-learning children and would help develop the ability to initiate the structure and experience of others, with the attendant opportunity for increased self-respect.

(f) The emphasis on the development of self-direction, persistence, low distractibility, and self-control (*e.g.*, the "silent" periods).

(g) The respect for the child explicit in the very physical structure of the Montessori classroom and in the assumption that the child will *enjoy* and spontaneously respond to the opportunities to learn.

(h) It would also be expected that the emphasis on individual development, on discipline of the mind and the body, and on the rights of others would facilitate the development of social adjustment in the child.

(i) In addition, there is little demand for verbal fantasy and "imaginativeness" in the real-world-orientated "tasks" in the Montessori classroom. In contrast to programs more oriented toward verbal elaborations and divergent production, the breakdown of these necessary life tasks into specific steps to be accomplished in sequence has the double benefit of training in practical activities the child should learn and of congruence with the slow-learning child's abilities in dealing with concrete materials. It is of interest that Montessori's insight into the role of preverbal cognitive systems is supported by studies that have demonstrated that language systems as we know them are not necessary for the accomplishment of quite complex discrimination, abstraction, and generalization tasks. Monkeys, for example, form "learning sets" in which the animals eventually learn on the first trial with two objects (say, a cookie cutter and a ball) which one is "right" for that set of trials, and will perform equally well with a new pair (say, a plastic cup and a pencil) after only the first trial for information. More recent studies with children between three and four years of age have also demonstrated that in the absence of verbalization, and without training in specific verbal cues, such concepts as "middle size" and "pointed" can be transferred to quite complex visual stimuli. There is no question, of course, of the importance of language skills for communication and facilitation of planful "If . . . then" reasoning. I am suggesting that other lines of research confirm Montessori's identification of sensory-discrimination and attentional capacities as primary and support the hypothesis that training in language skills should be coordinated with the child's basic cognitive skill attainment.

(j) Still another aspect of the Montessori approach that is congruent with the characteristics of the slow-learning child is the opportunity for comprehensive exploration and consolidation of skills by repetition. The apparent brief memory span of the slow learner means that more trials will be needed for internalization of the skill; Montessori tasks have been reported to stimulate great persistence in solving the task and a spontaneous desire for prolonged repetition following the first correct solution. There seems to be little known about the whys of this striking observation. One possibility is that what seems to us repetition may be discovery to the child, as a different nuance of shape, sequence, or relationship is noticed. Some children may be able to abstract a great deal in a few experiences; the "brief memory span" of the slow learner may reflect inadequate retention of what is attended to in each experience coupled with relative limitations in what the child is actually perceiving.

To summarize: Montessori techniques emphasize sequential development (at the child's own pace) of sensorimotor discriminations, basic reasoning processes, specific practical skills, and complex reasoning and exploratory skills. The technique involves (a) the child's spontaneous interest in the equipment and activities; (b) persistence in problem solving and self-initiated "repetition"; and (c) the development of such character traits as self-control, self-confidence, and respect for the rights of others.

These characteristics are not all unique, of course, to the Montessori approach. The work of at least two other researchers may be mentioned: Skinner ("behaviorist") and Piaget ("cognitive"). The Skinnerian approach also emphasizes (a) careful sequencing of materials toward a clearly specific goal behavior; (b) the importance of the emitted response, originated by the child, as contrasted to the elicited or demanded response (and the corollary need for great patience on the part of the teacher or "experimenter"); and (c) the importance of the overt response, as contrasted to the internalized or symbolic response.

A "behaviorist" approach differs from Montessori techniques in at least two important ways:

(1) "Behaviorists" develop response-reward sequences to bring the behavior under sharp external control, as contrasted to the emphasis on intrinsic motivation, curiosity, and exploration which has interested other theorists. Montessori's approach would seem to combine this most transcendent of capacities—to explore, to be curious, to be rewarded by competence and achievement—with the structure and goal orientation that behaviorists have shown to be important for efficient learning. (It should also be mentioned that other learning theorists interpret the role of reward in the learning process to be "information.") In either context, the importance of immediate feedback regarding the correctness of response seems to be well established. Most Montessori materials provide for this feedback because the incorrect response does not permit completion of the task; for example, placing cutout pieces into a puzzle can be accomplished with a variety of response sequences but only one

correct piece/edge complex signals itself if the teacher's criterion of "all pieces included and a flat surface" is shared by the child.

(2) The behaviorist approach differs from the Montessori approach in still another way: on the utilization of successive approximation of response and the careful sequencing of tasks so that no failure is experienced. Observation of some Montessori equipment suggests that the materials have not been simplified so as to take advantage in the very earliest stages of the principle of "reward for the first smallest approximation of the response desired."[3] There is considerable disagreement, however, on the importance of a continually successful experience, as contrasted with the motivation possibly associated with (a) a sense of difficulty and cognitive conflict, and (b) the fact that the real world is not programmed so that failure is avoided: "It is more complex than that."

The second theorist I will mention is Piaget. One aspect of Piaget's work involves the identification of five phases in the child's cognitive development. As Piaget and his colleagues observed them, these are (1) the sensorimotor phase (about zero to two-and-one-half years); (2) the preconceptual phase (two-and-one-half to four-and-one-half years); (3) the phase of intuitive thought (about four-and-one-half to eight-and-one-half years); (4) the phase of concrete operations (about nine-and-one-half to twelve-and-one-half years), and (5) the phase of formal operations (about thirteen-and-one-half years on).[4] Note that as late as nine to twelve years, the inferences made by bright and normal children are influenced by the perceptual ("concrete operations") aspect of the situation and that skill in logical manipulation (the "If ... then" that questions perception) may not develop until after thirteen-and-one-half, a time sequence that is congruent with the twelve-year "leveling off" and the handicap in abstract reasoning reported as characteristic of the slower child. Note also the assumption that attainment of a later phase *depends* on the development of earlier phases (*e.g.*, perception-based inference cannot occur until the child has learned certain intuitive operations and skills of perceptual analyses).

It is in the massive body of observation and interpretations offered by Piaget that one major challenge to the Montessori approach may be posed. Some of the cognitive-perceptual skills in which the retarded child is deficient appear to be vital to the development of the reasoning capacities described by Piaget. Do the Montessori materials and sequencing take into account this information? Fascinating as the available materials and activities are, they seem oriented more toward specific information-skill goals than to the conceptual stages described by Piaget as underlying the acquisition of such content.

Another area of challenge is whether the Montessori materials will engage the slow-learning child as they do the normal or the deprived child. I emphasize materials and activities because much of the reported success of the Montessori approach with normal, bright and deprived children appears to depend on the attractiveness of these educational "toys" to these children, on the appropriate sequencing of steps, and on the relevance of the discriminations and skills developed to the child's world. While it is possible that few modifications would be necessary, we cannot assume that the slow-learning child will respond optimally to the existing exercises and equipment. He may need different tasks, oriented to the specific intellectual and social difficulties he faces; he may require intermediate steps in complexity and approximation approaches to certain exercises. And if the tasks are "broken down" we move from one complexity to another (*e.g.*, "return materials" in the table-washing task to "wring out cloth, hang up cloth, empty bucket, open cabinet door, replace bucket, close cabinet door") with consequently greater demands for retention and more requirements for "repetition" and great patience.

Despite the promise of Montessori techniques, there are few studies in the literature reporting the application of these approaches to slow-learning children. A sampling of recent texts in the field yielded only a few who mentioned Montessori, and these in historical reference. One exception is Argy's report[5] that handicapped children attained more in Montessori than in "traditional" classes. His study may become a classic example of experimental rigor in the naturalistic setting: the diagnoses of the children were clearly stated; comparable "Montessori" and traditional control groups were contrasted; and the criterion measures were based on general developmental expectations, *e.g.*, language skills, as well as the sensorimotor skills, where Montessori techniques might be expected to be particularly facilitating. There were, however, no children in this study who were "slow learners" without physical handicaps. National information is apparently not available, but an informal survey of Washington-area Montessori schools indicated that these were directed toward the middle-class bright child. While an occasional "slower child" was considered for admission, little effort was reported in developing the Montessori potential for this group—it was "sink or swim" for the individual child.

It seems ironic that Montessori originally was impressed by the fact that the retarded children whose training she supervised performed as well as normal children on standardized tests. This directed her attention to the potential for development apparently being lost in the normal child, a direction seemingly in evidence today. There appears to be an as yet unrealized opportunity for research in the development of new educational approaches integrating Montessori, behaviorist, and Piagetian approaches to the slow-learning child.

Among the possibilities for such research are (1) comparisons of "standard" Montessori and traditional approaches with such careful experimental methods as Argy's; (2) based on observations and results of these studies, modification of the Montessori materials and sequencing to take into account Piagetian and other research on developmental sequences, to be followed by a recycling of the comparison of "revised" Montessori and "traditional" approaches; (3) exploration of the possibilities of very early identification and training of slow-learning children by the Montessori techniques; and (4) studies of Montessori techniques for the *older* slow-learning individual.

Such a program could not be reasonably undertaken by a private school. Possibly one reason why Montessori approaches have not received research attention equivalent to the essay-type interest (of which this is an example) is that identification and training of the slow-learning child typically does not begin until the child is of school age and the Montessori approach is more widely developed for preschool, three-to-six-year-old children, who are usually educated privately, than it is for older children.

Considering the potential Montessori techniques seem to hold for the slow-learning child, one hopes for a large-scale program of systematic research perhaps along the outline described above. Another resource may be the opportunities for the parent and individual teacher to incorporate some of the ideas I have discussed.[6] Some possibilities are:

1. Know yourself and the child. Evaluate his skills and development on the basis of specific behavioral attainments, preferably from the structure of developmental theory (for example, mastery of *what* specific steps in self-care operations, knowledge of *what* physical characteristics of the world). Record the child's current level of development, identify appropriate educational goals, and work specifically toward these. Trace the child's progress, recycling evaluation, training, and evaluation. There are unfortunately few standardized developmental scales to guide you and none generally available that are based on Piaget's work or on the Montessori sequences. You will have to read the available research studies, visit Montessori classrooms, note the child's performance with materials you construct or borrow, and then yourself observe carefully what the child's spontaneous activities and vocalizations suggest about his developmental status.

2. Depending on the child's development (and I am, obviously, thinking of the younger child), focus on sensory differentiation, categorization, and oral communication. For example, obtain samples of many kinds of materials, encourage the child to feel them, to sort them, to categorize them simply. Obtain (or build) simple equipment that permits the concrete demonstration of certain concepts such as up–down right–left; larger, middle size, smaller— e.g., a cube with arrow cutouts that move to fit in; a form board with tin cans of various sizes that the child can place in proper sequence. Develop equipment that will encourage awareness of basic relationships, and task sequences of a practical nature.

3. Have these materials available to the child in labeled, open shelves. Encourage use of these materials in the atmosphere of "freedom with responsibility." Only work-oriented behavior should be encouraged when and where the child is using the materials. When the child becomes distracted, encourage structure by making

a clearly discriminable shift of activities so that time and place for "large motor activity" does not become confused with that for "work on materials." Provide a simple verbal structure: "Here we work. Here we eat. Here we swing."

4. "Repetition" seems to be needed for the slow-learning child. Have relatively few materials available for each educational goal, but let these be flexible to provide graded difficulty sequences and opportunities for transfer of concepts to different objects. For example, start your form board with two holes and with a very big and a very little tin can, increasing gradually the number of holes and tin cans. Then transfer the ordering skill to other objects, *e.g.*, two-dimensional materials, or length from height, and to materials that present some conflict between the materials and internalized expectations, *e.g.*, deeper holes so that equal-length pins do not line up. Encourage attention to different aspects of the materials, while emphasizing the relevance of the "correct" dimension. For example, "Shiny. Smooth. Big fits here; little fits there."

5. Coordinate verbal stimulation with sensorimotor activity. Keep the sentences simple and repeat the words frequently; direct the child's attention to the concept you wish to develop. For example, "This one is the bigger can and this one is the smaller can. Do you see? Now you do it," has much extraneous "noise" to a brief message. The two essential words are "bigger" and "smaller." Rely more on demonstration than direction, while sequencing verbalization as you would sensorimotor materials.

These are just a few suggestions. As you read and observe, think of what you could do within the home or classroom situation. Keep it simple so as not to overwhelm the child with a flood of ideas and enthusiasm, and then, if he flounders, a drought. Record what you have observed and done, for these observations could be valuable in developing more systematically the promise of Montessori for the slow-learning child.

LOIS-ELLIN DATTA

REFERENCES

[1] R.C. Orem, ed., *Montessori for the Disadvantaged* (New York, Putnam's, 1967).

[2] References on the slow-learning child include Christine P. Ingram, *Education of the Slow Learning Child*, 3rd ed. (New York, The Ronald Press, 1960); Samuel A. Kirk and G. Orville Johnson, *Educating the Retarded Child* (Boston, Houghton Mifflin, 1951); G. Orville Johnson, *Education for the Slow Learner* (Englewood Cliffs, N.J., Prentice-Hall, 1953); N.C. Kephart, *The Slow Learner in the Classroom* (Columbus, Ohio, Charles E. Merrill, 1960); and W.M. Cruickshank, ed., *Psychology of Exceptional Children and Youth* (Englewood Cliffs, N.J., Prentice-Hall, 1963). A bulletin by William A. Lynch, *Instructional Objectives and the Mentally Retarded Child* (Indiana University, Bureau of Educational Studies and Testing, 1967) provides a readable, stimulating discussion of the implications of current research in learning, motivation and child development.

[3] Three inexpensive and informative references are Lillian C. Howitt, *Creative Techniques for the Slow Learner* (Englewood Cliffs, N.J., Prentice-Hall, 1964); W.B. Featherstone, *Teaching the Slow Learner* (New York, Teacher's College, Columbia University, 1951), and Jack Abramowitz, *Diary of a Slow Learner Class* (Chicago, Follett, 1963).

[4] The *Journal of the Experimental Analysis of Behavior* publishes many articles concerned with approaches to learning that have developed from behaviorism. The *Journal of Experimental Research in Child Development* is another source of this material. Discussions of learning theories and the retarded child will be found in N.R. Ellis, ed., *Handbook of Mental Deficiency* (New York, McGraw-Hill, 1963) and other books edited by Ellis. See Mary Woodward, "The Application of Piaget's Theory to Research in Mental Deficiency," in N.R. Ellis, *op. cit.*, pp. 297–324; and W.B. Stephens, Piaget, and Inhelder—application of theory and diagnostic techniques to the area of mental retardation—*Education and Training of the Mentally Retarded*, 1, 1966, 75–86. The journal *Child Development* is a source of recent research on Piaget. A comprehensive presentation of Piaget's work is offered by John H. Flavell, *The Developmental Psychology of Jean Piaget* (New York, D. Van Nostrand, 1963). See also Henry W. Maier, *Three Theories of Child Development* (New York, Harper & Row, 1965). Flavell notes that replications of Piaget's observations may yield scales for precise developmental descriptions but at present, applications to evaluation, curricula, and teaching methods should be made cautiously.

[5] Argy.

[6] Don and Rosetta Rietz, "Linking the School with the Home," in R.C. Orem, *op. cit.*, pp. 117–134. The journal *Children's House* is a primary source of reports on recent experiences with Montessori techniques.

IV

Montessori Applications and
Techniques in Special Education

INSIGHTS

1. One of Montessori's most important contributions to education was to develop, using observation and experimentation, the "prepared environment" and "didactic material" making auto-education possible.

2. The indirect teaching of the Montessori directress stimulates activity and work on the part of the child; direct teaching by traditional teachers encourages immobility and passivity.

3. The Montessori directress helps the development of the child's inner-, active-, self-discipline; the traditional teacher often relies upon external discipline.

4. Work (positive experience) in a prepared environment can exert a "normalizing" influence upon the deviated child. "Work" is essential to the normal development of all children.

5. The young child learns and develops through "experiences upon the environment"; he experiments, explores, discovers, and masters.

6. Adults are "living didactic objects"—a most important feature of the environment; because the young child learns much by the process of imitation, the child should be exposed to exemplary adult behavior and language.

7. Montessori, first in special education and then working with normal children, developed muscular or motor education to enhance the optimum development of coordinated movements such as walking and breathing.

8. The child displays a sensitive period for developing body imagery—which involves learning the parts of his body, their positions and mastery, in relation spatially to the world about him.

9. The child's love of touching things in the process of learning

reflects the importance of the tactile sense; this importance is not yet sufficiently recognized or utilized in education.

10. Said Montessori: "The best teachers for children are children themselves." Freedom in her "ungraded" situation encourages children to learn from one another.

11. The "inner preparation" of teachers of young children is vital because "spirit" is more important in teaching than mechanical skill.

12. The teacher must attempt to rid herself of any qualities that would constitute an obstacle to the development of her children and to their acquisition of independence.

13. The "new education" is an experimental, child-centered pedagogy, consisting of aid given to child life, from birth.

14. The "new teacher" is "the patient one," who prepares an environment that fosters the child's natural development.

15. In the "new education," human potential now latent will be revealed and realized.

16. The child's "great work" is to build a man.

No one is better qualified to speak on Montessori matters than Lena Gitter (see her earlier selection). Educated in Vienna, where she received her Montessori training and opened a Montessori school, she fled the Nazis in 1938. Married to a physician, she has since replicated many of the pioneering educational endeavors of Maria Montessori. For example, just as the latter in her Casa dei Bambini experience worked with the poor, culturally impoverished child, so has Mrs. Gitter worked with such children for the Child Development Group of Mississippi.

She has made a number of study trips to different parts of the world to investigate the Montessori applications in various cultures. She has trained teachers and paraprofessionals in Montessori techniques, and serves as a roving evaluator for the American Montessori Society. Her daughter and son-in-law operate a Montessori school in Baltimore.

In this selection Mrs. Gitter discusses a number of important Montessori activities concepts including:

The Fundamental Lesson
Walking the Line
The Silence Game
Order, the Prepared Environment, and Exercises of Practical
   Life
The Three-Period Lesson

She summarizes her presentation with an interesting example of a practical implementation of Montessori.

MONTESSORI ACTIVITIES

THE FUNDAMENTAL LESSON

The array of exciting Montessori material by itself provides no guarantee of optimum learning with normal or special children. Needed in addition are certain teaching techniques that are used at every level in the Montessori class, beginning with the motor exercises and continuing through the sensorial to the academic work. The retarded, brain-damaged, or emotionally disturbed child presents a variety of special problems that must be met before positive learning can take place. For example, the child may be easily upset by the presence of extraneous objects, or by the stimulation of too many words, because he lacks the ability to discriminate between the relevant and irrelevant stimuli. Therefore, ways must be found to isolate the material we wish him to learn, by creating an environment that won't distract him from the material to be learned.

Specifically, the table where the child is to work may have to be cleared of objects such as plants and other decorations that form such a pleasant background for the normal child, but which may distract the special child. The teacher's movements as she arranges the table and other furniture should be quiet and simple. The chair is placed gently by the table. The teacher then walks gracefully to where the material to be used in the lesson is kept. She shows the material to the child and demonstrates how to carry it to his work space. She should make certain that the child shows interest in the work. If he doesn't, she will wait for a more opportune moment, the "teachable moment," and proceed from the beginning again.

After the material is placed properly on the otherwise empty table, the lesson begins. The child may work with his material for as long as he wishes, after the directress has demonstrated its correct use. Rather than use complicated verbal directions, the teacher will utilize appropriate gestures at an unhurried pace to show what is to be done. She should then refrain from offering additional comments or assistance until the child requests help.

With the special child a great deal of initial "showing" may be necessary, but the teacher should not unnecessarily repeat demonstrations. Rather, she should wait patiently until the child reveals a need for further instruction. The teacher must be sure to first demonstrate the primary purpose of the material, saving all of the interesting variations possible for a later time, which will be signaled by the expressed interest of the child. When the lesson is completed, the material is returned to its proper place on the shelf by the child as soon as he has learned to do so.

The technique of the fundamental lesson, as described above, is basic to all learning in the Montessori classroom, and prepares the child for the ever-more-challenging tasks that follow its mastery.

WALKING THE LINE

Exercises that lead to improved muscular coordination should be a regular part of any Montessori class, including those for the special child. Walking the line is such an exercise.

A line in the form of an oval is marked on the floor with chalk or masking tape (if a permanent painted line is not allowed). It should be about an inch wide, and can enclose as large an area as the room permits. (A smaller second oval can be placed within it for children with more severe coordination problems.)

The children space themselves equidistant on the line and,

following the teacher's example, walk on the line, gradually taking smaller and smaller steps until they are walking heel-to-toe in a slow and regular rhythm. Music can be played, if desired. When the children have mastered this basic exercise, various modifications can be introduced to refine muscular skills already learned.

Children can use flashlights to throw a beam on the line before them, or carry small flags held high to encourage walking with head up—first one flag, then two. Objects can be balanced on their heads without using hands. Bells that must be carried without tinkling, or small glasses of colored water that must not spill can be introduced. Each modification represents a challenge; each challenge mastered, a victory; each victory, a "step forward" in the child's education.

THE SILENCE GAME

The "silence game" or "lesson of silence" is another "simple" exercise that accomplishes several purposes, and has the advantage of requiring no special equipment. The child learns self-control over muscles and bodily movements as he does when "walking the line"—control that is often so difficult for the special child to achieve.

The teacher rings a small bell to gain the children's attention, or she may utilize a fishbowl or other interesting object to focus their attention. She may establish silence by writing the word "Silence" on the board, by speaking the word ever more quietly, or by setting an example through her own silence.

Gradually, as the room falls silent, the children seat themselves at their tables, moving the chairs softly, composing themselves for relaxation, each child assuming a position in which he will be comfortable without moving about. Awareness of muscles and their control promotes the quiet performance of these activities.

Slowly, each child relaxes and is still, aware perhaps for the first time of the variety and persistence of background noises: a watch ticking, a bird chirping, the curtain rustling. This may be a novel experience for a child in our culture, with its transistor radios, TV, and piped-in music. Silence can have an emotional or spiritual significance for all, but especially for the special child, who often lives in what for him is a confusion of noises. Silence, then, as not merely the absence of noise but, as a positive sensory experience, can offer a degree of tranquillity. When coupled with practice in muscular self-control it becomes doubly beneficial for the special child.

In addition, the silence game can provide valuable preparation for adult life, which may require moving and working in relative quiet, and prolonged concentration, as in listening. The child who has learned to compose himself, to observe silence, may go with his family to a movie or musical performance where such self-control is required.

When the room is silent and each child is motionless, the teacher rises gracefully and walks quietly to one end of the room. Then, speaking softly, she calls each child by name. She may want to dim the lights or draw the blinds to heighten the stillness. The child who is called rises, places his chair at the table, and walks to the teacher, who waits to give him a smile—a smile meant just for him.

Children, in general, enjoy the silence that is necessary for hearing their names whispered, and respond with pleasure to the sound. For the special child, who frequently has problems of identification, this acknowledgment of his name and presence has unusual appeal.

ORDER, THE PREPARED ENVIRONMENT, AND EXERCISES OF PRACTICAL LIFE

Usually, in a prepared environment, children quickly assume responsibility for helping to create and maintain physical order, and the teacher's role can be minimized. However, the children at times will need assistance; the adult must learn to judge the situation and give assistance when it is required, in a pleasant, quiet, self-assured way. When she observes that a child is overtired or unduly stimulated she must understand the need for flexibility in applying the classroom rules. She may, for example, decide to help the child return his materials to the shelf, rather than insist that he return them by himself. If she thinks, however, that her authority is being tested in such a situation she may have difficulty helping. She should remember, then, that one of her primary goals is the preservation of order and serenity, not the imposition of her will.

Deciding when and to what degree to intervene is not an easy task for the Montessori teacher, or for any teacher, of normal or special children. But the "prepared environment" will help the Montessori teacher to maintain the necessary atmosphere of order.

The "prepared environment" implies a place for everything and everything in its place, with responsibility for "placing" shared by teacher and children. The resulting order helps the child (and the teacher) feel more secure. The children will come to look forward to all the jobs necessary for keeping the room attractive and orderly.

These "housekeeping tasks" are one type of practical life exercise, and can be a source of great emotional satisfaction for children who have experienced too little success. They enjoy performing again and again tasks involving the care of the classroom: washing, polishing, sweeping, dusting, etc.

These duties encourage a sense of responsibility, of pride in work well done, of pleasure in the orderly environment, while developing increasing eye-hand coordination on all levels from the simple to complex. The child learns to perceive the differences between a clean chair and a dirty one and to take pride in his work, the work that accomplishes a change so clearly visible to himself and others.

As the quality of the teacher's intervention (and therein lies her art, says Montessori) improves with practice, she will be rewarded by success. The children will increasingly display confidence in themselves, responding positively to the environment and to her. They, in short, will learn!

THE THREE-PERIOD LESSON—AN EXAMPLE

Basically, the three-period lesson breaks the learning of new material into three steps. In teaching the first two letters of the alphabet, for example, the teacher offers to the child "A" and "B," perhaps in the form of "sandpaper letters" pasted on cardboard squares. Only these two letters are placed in the child's view, as the teacher enunciates clearly and slowly, "A, A, A," pointing to the letter and allowing the child to see, feel, and hear the letter "A." Then he repeats "A, A, A," the teacher observing carefully for any sign of a hearing problem or speech difficulty as she evaluates his response. She again identifies the letter, and the child repeats the letter after her. Such repetition continues until the child has mastered the association between the letter form and sound. The same procedure is followed with the letter "B."

In the second period, with both sandpaper letters "A" and "B" on the table, the teacher asks the child: "Give me 'A,'" or "Give me 'B.'" The letters are then rearranged and the teacher asks again. If the child is unable to distinguish between the two letters, the teacher patiently returns to the first period of the lesson for additional reinforcement before trying the second period again.

When the child can do the first and second periods without error he is ready for the third period, in which he must remember the name himself and pronounce it correctly. The teacher picks up one letter and asks, "What is this?" If the child identifies it correctly, she presents the other letter. If necessary, she returns to the second period for review. When the child consistently answers correctly, this particular three-period lesson—involving only the letters "A" and "B"—is complete.

On the following day, new letters may be introduced, but each lesson should start with some familiar material.

The three-period lesson offers a number of advantages for teaching the special child. By limiting the material to be learned at any one time, it provides a focus of interest for the child and permits a close check on error. When, for example, the child does not give the correct response, the teacher is quickly alerted, as the mistake has not been lost amidst a welter of other learning experiences. She can often isolate problems and return to an earlier stage of the lesson to review a particular point.

The concrete Montessori materials, which lead to the more difficult abstractions, make it possible for the teacher to observe the child's progress from noncomprehension to comprehension.

LENA L. GITTER (WITH R. C. OREM)

A MONTESSORI MARCH OF DIMES

Every teacher can acquire equipment—durable but not expensive —for cleaning and maintenance of the classroom. This equipment can be used imaginatively to help the child develop a variety of practical skills. For example, ordinary shoe-shining materials provided an exciting adventure in learning for mentally retarded children in a Maryland elementary school.

My chairmanship of a March of Dimes campaign had motivated the two special classes in the school to earn money to donate to this cause. Their earning task was an outgrowth of a Montessori practical life exercise adopted earlier—that of polishing shoes. The children had enjoyed doing their own and often asked to polish the teachers' shoes as well. When we showed a film about the March of Dimes and discussed the campaign with our children, they voted to assume the responsibility of earning money by setting up a little shoeshine shop.

We advertised the enterprise by making and distributing leaflets to the entire school, using language and art to develop our motto: "A Shine in Time Will Provide a Dime for the March of Dimes." The children assembled and prepared the brushes and various colors of shoe polish on linoleum-covered tables. Older girls made cobbler-type aprons for the boys while other children became cashiers, learning valuable lessons in handling money and making correct change. A large chart was posted showing the number of shoes shined and the amount of money earned each day.

My class of younger educable mentally retarded, aged seven to ten, did not match the production of the older children, of course, but they were able to set up a special display consisting of shoes of different colors, materials, and styles. They had not realized there were so many kinds of shoes, and work with the display proved an important learning experience.

This interesting collection attracted much attention when it was moved to the display case in the school's central hall. The children began to think and talk about the shoes that their fathers had seen or used during military service in different parts of the world: Chinese clogs, wooden and fur shoes, Austrian boots. Our special class pupils "stepped out of their own shoes" as it were, and into a wider world as they became aware of distant peoples and countries, using a map and globe to locate them geographically.

We used many stories and poems about shoes while our "business" was operating. The children responded especially to "The Red Clogs" by Masako Matsuno, which is about a little Japanese girl who ruins her new red clogs playing in water. There was also much opportunity for artwork, including the viewing of slides on art. The children were quite impressed with Van Gogh's painting "The Old Shoes." The music teacher featured songs about shoes, and with her help the students created a little play about shoemakers.

The director of the March of Dimes accepted the money the children had earned—and quite impressive it was, too: $36.50 in small change—just as it had been received!

This project, with all of its ramifications, is but one example of what children can do within the atmosphere that a Montessori-oriented classroom can offer. Here children find themselves in an environment that, by offering practical life exercises and other confidence-building situations, is suited to their abilities.

The special child, often frustrated in the regular academic class through repeated failure, learns that in a Montessori environment he is not competing with anyone, but can work at his own pace. And the work he is doing is not dependent upon highly sophisticated verbal communication.

LENA L. GITTER (WITH R. C. OREM)

THE "DIFFERENT" CHILD—WITH EMPHASIS UPON MONTESSORI

SELECTED READINGS, BRIEFLY ANNOTATED

Amos, Wm., and Orem, R.C., *Managing Student Behavior*. St. Louis, Mo., Warren H. Green, 1967.

   Practical handbook rooted in Montessori principles, especially for new primary and secondary teachers, and for inner-city teachers.

Children's House. P.O. Box 111, Caldwell, N.J.

A popular periodical with articles about Montessori and other approaches.

Cort, H.R., Commins, W., Henderson, N., and Orem, R.C., *A Study of the Full-Year 1966 Head Start Programs.* Prepared for the Office of Economic Opportunity, Project Head Start, Division of Research and Evaluation, Washington, D.C., 1967.

Probably the most comprehensive evaluation of the effects of Head Start done to date.

Gitter, Lena, *Montessori and Special Education.* Seattle, Wash., Special Child Publications, 1968.

Application of Montessori philosophy and techniques to special education.

———, "Montessori: Direction for Head Start," in *Montessori for the Disadvantaged*, R.C. Orem, ed. New York, Putnam's, 1967.

In addition to Mrs. Gitter's selection, there are selections by J.E. Wallin, Norris Haring, J. McV. Hunt, R. Buckminster Fuller, G.N. Getman, and others.

———, *Montessori Approach to Special Education.* Washington, D.C., Lena Gitter, 1966.

Influence of Itard and Seguin on Montessori, and implications of Montessori for special education in the 1960's.

———, *Montessori in Mississippi: Summer, 1966.* Washington, D.C., Lena Gitter, 1966.

Training of subprofessionals in Montessori theory and practice, for the Child Development Group of Mississippi.

———, "Art in a Class for Mentally Retarded Children." *Bulletin of Art Therapy*, Vol. 3, 1964.

Art possibilities for the special child, in an environment prepared along Montessori lines.

Montessori, Maria, *The Absorbent Mind.* Adyar, Madras 20, India, Theosophical Pub. House, 1961.

Montessori's classic statement of the psychology and learning of early childhood.

O'Keefe, A., and Orem, R.C., "Research Problems in Evaluating Preschool Programs for Culturally Disadvantaged Youth." *National Catholic Kindergarten Review.* Winter, 1967.

How the researcher can recognize and deal with the normal and "special" problems found in the evaluation of preschool programs for deprived youth.

Orem, R.C., "Language and the Culturally Disadvantaged," in *Counseling the Disadvantaged Youth*, W. Amos and J. Grambs, eds. Englewood Cliffs, N.J., Prentice-Hall, 1968.

Why the informal language of the culturally deprived differs fundamentally from formal English, and how youth and counselors can communicate.

————, and Stevens, G., "Montessori and Language Development," *National Catholic Kindergarten Review*. March, 1968.

Fifty Montessori insights related to the young child's language learning are briefly explained.

————, *A Montessori Handbook*. New York, Putnam's, 1965.

Text of *Dr. Montessori's Own Handbook*, with contributors from various disciplines. See the review of this book in *Children Limited*, published by the National Association for Retarded Children, Vol. 15, No. 4. 1966.

Stevens, George, and Orem R.C., *The Case for Early Reading*. St. Louis, Mo., Warren H. Green, 1967.

How preschoolers can benefit from informal exposure to beginning reading, with a chapter on "Montessori and Early Learning."

R. C. OREM
LENA L. GITTER

SOME MONTESSORI OBSERVATIONS

Rosetta Rietz, the Montessori directress who organized the first Montessori class for brain-damaged children in the Midwest, has experimented with various learning environments for brain-injured children. She had theorized originally that, because of their "distractibility," such children would adjust best to a relatively neutral environment containing few children and limited visual and auditory stimuli. However, careful observation of and comparison between two classes she directed changed her thinking.

The first daily three-hour class had an enrollment of thirty-four normal children and only one brain-injured child. The second class, also in session for three hours daily, was conducted for eight brain-injured children.

She noticed that several very significant elements found in the first class were essentially lacking in the second group. These were: (1) spontaneity, (2) peer instruction (children teaching and learning from each other), and (3) group interaction and social dynamics. Since these elements comprise the heart of a Montessori class, she decided to form a class with equal numbers of normal and brain-injured children when the opportunity presented itself.

When this class finally materialized, it contained seventeen normal and seventeen brain-injured children with an age range from *two-and-one-half years through fifteen years*.

Neurological impairment ranged from mild to severe. The brain-injured youngsters displayed a variety of language, motor, visual-perceptual, and auditory-perceptual problems of varying degree. There was considerable hyperactivity and disorganization. At the outset, all the brain -injured children had difficulty in concentration and self-control. Several had already been dismissed from nursery schools and kindergartens, three from special education classes, six from first grade, and three from second grade.

But gradually, one by one, they became aware of the environment, the ground rules, the materials, and the other children in the class. Sometimes, another child would offer direct help or a word of correction.

Limits were gradually understood. The freedom to choose one's own work was appreciated. The challenges of the Montessori materials captured the attention of the brain-injured youngsters, who began to complete "cycles of work." The demands of these materials are realistic enough to be met—neither so easy as to produce boredom, nor so difficult as to result in frustration.

Through daily and continuous activity with one piece of material at a time the brain-injured children proved that they could learn to concentrate in the stimulating environment of a Montessori class-room. Only after they had become spontaneously and deeply involved in work did behavioral changes occur.

Results from this class over a period of time have led to the following conclusions:

1. Brain-injured children can function adequately in a large mixed group.

2. Brain-injured children can learn to concentrate in a Montessori-type environment. Extraneous stimuli can be excluded by fixing their attention on one piece of work or activity at a time.

3. Brain-injured children can learn in a highly stimulating environment.

4. Brain-injured children learn acceptable social behavior quickly from the example of their normal peers.

5. Brain-injured children have a greater potential for learning than most teachers realize. They need normal models to observe and imitate to help tap this learning potential.

6. Normal children are not adversely affected by the presence of brain-injured children. A balanced population prevents this. Normal children do acquire such human qualities as:

   (a) *compassion* for a fellow human being's misfortune

   (b) *understanding* of the differences and likenesses between all human beings

   (c) *respect* for the worth and dignity of all fellow human beings

   (d) *gratitude* for the gift of a whole body

   (e) *wisdom* in using the gift for the benefit and welfare of self and humanity

ROSETTA RIETZ

The following candid observations are intended to give some hint of what can be seen in one of Mrs. Rietz's Montessori classrooms with mixed normal and special children.

In February, the directress brought to the classroom an inset puzzle of a tree showing the major parts of the tree: roots, trunk, etc. She gave a simple demonstration of assembling it to a group that had come spontaneously to watch.

This was really the first and the last such lesson given by her. New lessons were given to children who did not know how to work with the puzzle by the children who had watched her. As these children repeated the exercise, the other children learned by observing.

Spontaneity can be seen every day, in a wide variety of situations.

The directress, towel in hand, is about to clean up some water when Janette, who has been standing nearby watching, takes the towel from her hand—wordlessly—and does it herself.

The directress plays on a beautiful piano (which was donated to the class) as the children walk the line. Their pleasure in the music and this activity is so great that the group always applauds when she finishes playing.

In preparation for the line-walking exercise, the directress never has to make a formal announcement, or assemble and arrange the group. Her action in going to the piano and playing a particular piece is signal enough. Spontaneously, the entire group assembles in an orderly line and commences the exercise.

As the time for the morning snack approaches, the directress's initial preparations for this activity serve as a "call" to the children who, one by one, become aware of what is happening. They put away their work, then organize themselves for carrying out the tasks necessary for snack time.

There is no jostling or quarreling. Rarely, a piece of china may be broken, but such accidents are a valuable learning experience.

One of the most mature boys has assumed responsibility for lighting the candles placed on the tables.

In the first month of school, the directress demonstrated how to wash a small table.

One morning, later in the term, Leroy decided that he wanted to wash one of the large rectangular tables. The directress had watched Leroy's skills, interests, and sense of freedom grow, and his decision to tackle one of these heavy tables did not surprise her.

However, he found the table difficult to move, because of its weight. Another boy, who had been watching him, eagerly volunteered to help, and the two then shared the labor involved in this activity.

Even such a relatively "simple" or routine (measured by adult standards) task as table washing is enjoyed by the children. It involves a number of stages and affords both large and small muscle exercises. As was the case above, it can be a cooperative activity—a genuine exercise in social training—and provides the sense of accomplishment that so many children need.

The system of taking turns, of waiting to work with something another person has, is a planned feature of the Montessori classroom and one that proves to be appreciated by the children.

After the directress has introduced them to this system—this order—they earnestly and consistently attempt to adhere to it. In fact, they are quick to enforce the rule if someone tries to break it.

Learning to wait and to be patient is transferred to group activities that require it. The group then becomes a little society working together in order as when, for example, they set the table and serve at snack time.

It is interesting to observe how the children are able to determine the number of individuals who should participate in a particular activity, rather than disorganize and spoil it with too many workers.

Love of Order

The box holding pencils has become disorderly because some pencils were not returned to their proper place.

When this happens, a child, noticing the disorder, will take the box to a table and reorganize it.

A shelf becomes disorderly.

A child will, spontaneously, remove all the contents and replace them properly.

A water-pouring unit becomes dirty.

Self-motivated, a child cleans the unit and refills containers with fresh water.

A practical life corner becomes disorderly and cluttered, with wastepaper spilled on the floor.

One or perhaps two children will become aware of the condition and reorder the corner.

At the outset of a new class the children are shown that the Montessori "prepared environment" offers a number of freedoms. Children are free to work with the didactic materials and to engage in the most varied exercises; they can move about a class, explore the room, and they can talk to one another quietly; they can organize group activities or work alone.

They are also shown clearly and firmly that there are necessary limits to this freedom. A child may not, for example, harass another child or interfere with his work or freedom. Material may not be abused, and must be returned when work with it is finished.

In the matter of discipline, the Montessori directress has a number of elements to assist her: the lure of the attractiveness and order of the room and materials; the exercises and work encouraging the child to explore and become involved; the clarity of the ground rules; most important, the children's own energies and innate forces to learn channeled in constructive exercises.

The Montessori method is being used increasingly as the basic educational component in total treatment programs for special children. Since Montessori's concern as a physician-educator for the well-being of the "whole child" is reflected throughout her approach, it is not surprising that children's hospitals, treatment centers, and institutions are establishing Montessori educational programs for their clientele, or utilizing locally available Montessori facilities.

The following case history shows how the Montessori approach can complement the other programs of a treatment center providing services for a brain-injured child.

A CASE OF NEUROLOGICAL DYSORGANIZATION: RESULTS OF TREATMENT WITH A CYBERNETIC APPROACH AND A MONTESSORI ENVIRONMENT

> Montessori has, moreover, re-emphasized a number of vital educational principles, such as the principles of development—the unfolding of the child's latent impulses—and of individuality, previously emphasized by Locke, Rousseau, Froebel, and Seguin; the necessity for the individual study of children, particularly the need of observing their spontaneous behavior and interests, foreshadowed by Locke, Itard, and Seguin; and the importance of giving children freedom and liberty of action, emphasized by Rousseau and Froebel.*

Current interest in the Montessori movement in America has resulted in the founding of many classes and schools by groups of parents wanting to provide the best possible education for their children. While there has been some interest and activity in applying Montessori principles to the brain-injured child, most Montessori schools are operated primarily for normal children. There is a tendency to lose sight of the origins and evolution of the Montessori principles and methodology,[1] which stem from the work of Itard, Seguin, and their predecessors who dealt with defective children.[2]

In the years following World War II, Doman, Delacato,[3,4,5,6,7,8] and their co-workers began to experiment with a new and different approach to the treatment of children with brain injuries. This approach, which is an outgrowth of the pioneer work of Dr. Temple Fay and his colleagues, integrates very well with the work of Montessori and her predecessors, and has applications to both handicapped and normal children. The following is a report on a child who has had the advantages of both this cybernetic approach to treatment of brain injury *and* the benefit of Montessori principles

---

* J.E.W. Wallin, *The Education of Handicapped Children*. Boston, Houghton Mifflin, 1924, p. 21.

applied both at home and in a Montessori classroom geared specifically to the brain-injured child.

This child was born in 1963 after an induced labor that lasted one-and-a-half hours. She seemed normal although slightly sluggish. Jaundice developed, however, and an exchange transfusion was done at six days of age because of a rare type of blood incompatibility. Her general development seemed to progress satisfactorily although at times there were certain intangible suspicious factors. From age six weeks her mother was advised to allow her baby to be in a prone position on the floor and not to confine her to a chair or a playpen. She crawled at six-and-a-half months, crept on hands and knees at seven-and-a-half months, and walked at eighteen months. From six months until ten months she vomited much of her solid food and milk with a resultant loss of weight and strength, in spite of continual attempts at diagnosis and treatment. At ten months the vomiting suddenly ceased. Between eleven and twelve months she was admitted to the hospital for a stubborn kidney infection that was under treatment for several months. After discharge from the hospital at one year of age she contracted regular measles from a hospital exposure, and also had repeated upper-respiratory infections.

As time passed, it became apparent that her coordination was very poor and there was a definite lag in her speech development. She also was extremely hyperactive and was very prone to frequent violent tantrums. She was seen at a speech clinic at age three years and one month. Clinical examination results were as follows:

A. *General Clinical Impressions:* A broad-based stance and walking pattern gave the impression of a child younger than three years. Her attention was not easily focused or maintained, but she did show some improvement as examination proceeded.

B. *Hearing:* A formal audiometric test was not attempted because of age. She did respond to directions and her name at conversational loudness levels. She had an expressive vocabulary, which ruled out a serious hearing loss.

C. *Peripheral Speech Mechanism:* This was demonstrated to be normal in structure and function for vegetative purposes.

D. *Motor:* Tasks from the Oseratsky Motor Scale were attempted, but she could not appreciate the directions. In paper and pencil tasks it was observed that thumb opposition was not established. In general, muscle tone appeared minimal and coordination less efficient than age expectations.

E. *Intelligence:* On the Peabody Picture Vocabulary Test she scored at the mental age level of two years, ten months. On the Goodenough Draw-A-Man Test, her mental age was evaluated as three years. Geometric designs were correctly copied through the three-year level.

F. *Speech and Language:*

1. *Articulation:* A picture articulation test revealed a variety of omissions and distortions, and it was the estimation of the examiner that intelligibility of speech was poor. Voice quality was slightly hoarse.

2. *Language:* Eleven pictures out of eighteen were identified for a passing score at III Level on Picture Vocabulary Task, Binet Scale. Failures were scored for task *Obeying Simple Commands* and *Response to Pictures.*

The diagnosis of the examiner at the speech clinic, in summary, was: deficient motor coordination; delay in speech skills and atypical behavior patterns, probably from central nervous system injury. Intelligence thought to be normal but special help certainly needed.

She was seen with the above deficiencies at age thirty-eight months at the Chicago Center for Achievement of Human Potential. Here, in addition to a complete physical and neurological examination, functional tests were performed in mobility, language, manual competence, and also in the areas of visual, auditory, and tactile competence. As to her mobility, the lower stage of mobility development of crawling in a prone position was rated as poor. Her walking and running in a complete cross pattern likewise were rated as poor, and she exhibited no mobility skills such as hopping, skipping, and jumping, etc. In language, she used only two or three words consecutively for the most part, and these were spoken with very poor pronunciation. Manually, her thumb-finger opposition bilaterally and simultaneously was rated as poor and her bimanual function only as fair. There was no apparent visual acuity problem, but she had a mild divergent strabismus and her convergence of vision at near point was rated as poor. Her auditory competence was such that she was able to follow a two- or three-step command, and she showed understanding of household articles and where they were kept. She had no understanding of time concept. Her tactile competence enabled her to make tactile differentiations of a number of small objects that were similar but not identical. Aside from the above, her general physical and neurological examinations were essentially normal except for exaggerated deep-tendon reflexes.

A diagnosis was made of chronic brain syndrome resulting probably from a central nervous system injury due to the blood incompatibility and possibly aggravated by regular measles. There was also the possibility that the negative effects of a brain injury could have also been aggravated by her general environment in infancy. Her mother volunteered that because of the baby's poor start and constant illnesses, she had an unfavorable attitude toward the child. The mother's emotional involvement made it difficult for her to help or encourage the baby. She had not talked or played with the baby very much because the baby always seemed to be sick.

However complex the factors involved in the etiology, there was a definite problem that had to be rectified if the child were to achieve anything near her potential, which seemed to be at least that of average intelligence.

A treatment program was outlined that, first of all, called for structuring the environment at home along Montessori lines, which would provide maximum opportunity for self-help and purposeful beneficial sensory stimulation. The child was to have maximum opportunity for mobility and spend specified amounts of time every day in the lower stages of mobility development—namely, crawling in a prone position, and creeping on hands and knees. Also, these lower patterns of mobility development were externally applied to her for five minutes at a time four times a day. In addition to receiving speech therapy, she also carried out activities to enhance her language development such as chewing, blowing, and tongue and lip exercises. This was accomplished in a variety of informal ways, including providing her with food that would encourage the desired type of activity. In the three areas of motor development—mobility, language, and manual competence—the attained level of development was reinforced and attempts were made to promote the next higher level. In the manual area, a variety of practical life materials were used, such as the buttoning and other types of dressing frames. Other activities such as pouring, tracing, coloring, finger painting, screwing on bottle caps, and cutting were done to enhance thumb-finger opposition and bimanual function. Visual treatment consisted of a form of orthoptics to help improve the poor convergence at near point. Also, opportunity was given to help her differentiate various pictures and symbols within her experience. In addition, she did eye-tracking exercises through vertical, horizontal, circular, and diagonal planes, first with another person holding the object being followed and then with the child herself holding the object. For further auditory and visual stimulation, and also to help with visual language development, there were frequent short exposures to familiar body image and environmental words using the three periods of learning that are followed throughout in Montessori education. The same principle held true for the sensory side of the developmental profile that was used as a measuring instrument. That is, the attained level of development was reinforced and attempts were made to bring out the next higher level. Also, there was an intensified increase in sensory stimulation over all available pathways in order to greatly increase the input.

Systematic efforts were made to increase the quantity and quality of motor output and sensorimotor coordination, as well as the higher level of discrimination and thinking. In the tactile area, again much use was made of a variety of Montessori-type materials that could be used to good advantage at home and did not require the full Montessori classroom environment.

Other aspects of the treatment consisted of reducing the oral fluid intake, which previously had been up to two to three quarts a day. After determining that there was no contraindication to this step, the oral fluids were restricted to a total of twenty-eight ounces per day. Also, a breathing program was instituted that entailed breathing into a plastic mask for one minute out of each waking hour. The primary purpose of this was aimed at increasing the vital capacity and improving respiratory function. There is also the secondary benefit of possibly increasing cerebral circulation through increased carbon dioxide content.

Basically, this same treatment program, with some revisions, was continued. The child was seen at regular two-month intervals—the last time being in June, 1967, when she was fifty-and-one-half months of age. As time went by, improvements took place in mobility, language, and manual competence as well as in visual convergence and in understanding of spoken language. However, the extreme hyperactivity and extremely violent temper tantrums persisted and constituted real problems. At this point, after about ten months on the cybernetic treatment for her neurologic dysorganization, she was admitted to a Montessori classroom that had been established specifically for brain-injured children but which also had a number of normal children in attendance.

Within a short time there was a definite decrease in hyperactivity and in the violent temper tantrums that had been such a prominent part of her behavior. She soon began to show a greater capacity to observe differences, similarities, and gradations, and to learn from observation, imitation, and experiences. Some aspects of her treatment from the Chicago Center, such as the patterning and the breathing, were carried out in the school concurrently with the Montessori activities.

As noted, she was again seen at the center in June, 1967, and reevaluated on the developmental profile. At this time her mother reported that her hyperactivity had markedly diminished and that she now obeyed well at home and had been a completely changed individual in the two-and-a-half months since starting at the Montessori school. In addition to the improvement in behavior, there were definite improvements in the quality of her lower mobility activities and she was beginning to crawl in a fairly well-coordinated cross-pattern movement in a prone position. Also, her walking and running in a complete cross pattern now met the criteria of a fair rating, and she had begun to improve with respect to mobility skills. Her language had improved greatly as to the number of words in her vocabulary, the length of her sentences and questions, and their structure. The enunciation was still wanting, but overall marked changes had occurred. Manually, her thumb-finger opposition bilaterally and simultaneously was now good and her bimanual function rated as fair. Her convergence of vision was now good. In spite of frequent short exposures to large printed words, she still had limited recognition of them. Her understanding generally was good. Her tactile competence remained good, which it had been more or less from the beginning.

A report from the Montessori directress indicates that the child now moves about the classroom quickly, energetically, and with improved coordination in overall gross movements. She still needs some improvement in fine-muscle control in the hands and fingers. Her social interaction with the rest of the group has changed from clinging to the teacher for a good part of the day and becoming upset whenever another child touched her to a growing awareness of herself as an individual accepted by a group and able to respond accordingly. She enters into activities with some of the other children and is aware of the rules and limits of the classroom. She accepts them and complies with them almost to the point of making her critical of children who break the rules. Spontaneously, she participates in group activities and volunteers to perform in and for the group lessons. She is obedient and understands the authority of the directress with respect. This development of obedience reflects greater control of herself.

She is using the metal insets regularly, and the color tablet boxes. Also, she works with all four knobbed cylinder blocks, the pink tower, red stair, red rods, solid geometric shapes, dressing frames, and the matching and sorting exercises. She is able to identify seven geometric solids stereognostically and she can differentiate differences, similarities, sequences, and gradations in most of the sensorial materials she works with. She understands how the materials are to be used, and she works with them in the prescribed manner. She is developing an inner order by working more and more accurately with the sensorial materials; this inner order is also reflected in her pleasure at ordering the environment. In her language in the Montessori class she is learning to enunciate rather clearly and to express her ideas in complete sentences of twelve or more words.

Her overall progress in class has been excellent in view of the short time she has been in attendance. The directress, in her most recent report, is optimistic that this little girl will continue to develop favorably in the Montessori class.

The staff at the Chicago Center are of the opinion that progress should continue, and that, with further exposure to the combination of cybernetic treatment and a Montessori environment, both at home and in school, the child should eventually function very close to her potential, which appears to be that of at least average intelligence.

The results reported in this brief case history of but one child are similar to what is being accomplished with a group of other children with related or even worse handicaps. Some of these children had been dismissed from other schools for handicapped children as hopeless, and in some cases application had even been made for admission to an institution for residential care. There are, of course, a variety of dynamically interrelated factors in both the etiology and treatment of this particular child's difficulties, just as there are with these other children. Some of her problems seemed to stem from a poor emotional climate and sensory deprivation. No doubt, many other factors were involved. Whatever the causes contributing to her earlier condition, it is evident that there is a great need for more Montessori activity geared specifically to such brain-injured children and other handicapped children.

Montessori education, with its motor, sensory, and intellectual components, can complement other treatment being used for brain injury, and especially the Doman–Delacato approach. Montessori methodology can provide a responsive environment, both in the preschool and in the elementary age groups, for the great numbers of handicapped children who do not fit into any of the existing classes for mentally handicapped or normal children, and have found themselves in an educational no-man's-land.

PAUL J. DUNN, M.D.

REFERENCES

[1] William Boyd, *From Locke to Montessori*. New York, Henry Holt, 1914.

[2] R.C. Orem, ed., *Montessori for the Disadvantaged*. New York, Putnam's, 1967.

[3] Doman, R., Spitz, E., Zucman, E., Delacato, C.H., and Doman, G.: "Children With Severe Brain Injuries—Neurological Organization in Terms of Mobility." *Journal of the American Medical Association*, vol. 174. pp. 257–262, Sept. 17, 1960.

[4] LeWinn, E.B., Doman, G.J., Delacato, C.H., Doman, R.J., Spitz, E.B., and Thomas, E.W.: "Neurological Organization: The Basis for Learning" in *Learning Disorders*, Hellmuth, J., ed., Seattle, Wash.: Special Child Publications, 1966, pp. 51–93.

[5] LeWinn, E.B.: "Effect of Environmental Influences on Human Behavioral Development," *N.Y. State J. Med.* 66:3143–3145, (Dec. 15), 1966.

[6] LeWinn, E.B.: "The Measurement of Neurological Development." *Internat. J. Neuropsychiatry* (in press).

[7] Doman, R.J., Taylor, R.G., Jr., and Thomas, E.W.: "Brain Injury as a Diagnosis and the Results of Treatment in 335 Brain-Injured Children." *Developmental Medicine and Child Neurology* (in press).

[8] Thomas, E.W.: "The Validity of Brain Injury as a Diagnosis." *Human Potential*, Vol. 1, 1967 (in press).

As might be expected, Montessori schools differ widely with regard to physical plant, children served, programs offered, and other factors. The Montessori movement in America has tended to have the image of a fairly expensive middle to upper-middle class white suburban phenomenon. There are those who would argue that the children who need exposure to Montessori the most—the disadvantaged, for example—are least likely to receive it.

However, an increasing number of public and nonpublic schools (parochial, nonprofit, or for profit) are instituting Montessori in some form for children of many types: culturally disadvantaged, brain-damaged, emotionally disturbed, etc. Some of these schools offer scholarships to needy students.

Public school systems, such as Philadelphia is, are experimenting with the introduction of pilot Montessori classes directed by bona fide Montessori teachers. Some public schools house one or more Montessori classes for special children. But whatever the format, there appears to be growing awareness of Montessori possibilities on the part of public educators.

Some aspects of three diverse Montessori-type school programs are briefly described below.

* * * * *

Sister Domitilla Leonardi, teacher at Configliacchi Institute, in Padua, has written:

> I repeat then that practically all the material in use in the Montessori school for normal children can be very advantageously applied to the education of the blind, enabling them to receive in the imagination impressions which come the closest possible to reality and not levelled and uniform as is usual.

It is interesting to observe that Montessori prefaced her A Montessori Handbook *with a tribute to Helen Keller and her teacher, Mrs. Anne Sullivan Macy, noting that Helen Keller is "a marvelous example of the phenomenon common to all human beings: the possibility of the liberation of the imprisoned spirit of man by the education of the senses."*

The following selection is exerpted from a longer article that appeared in Today's Health *(February, 1967), published by the American Medical Association, and appears here with permission.*

THE SCHOOL WHERE BLIND CHILDREN "SEE"

My own fascination with Montessori concerns her discovery of the sensory modalities. The media are extensions of these.*

Hand in swinging hand, two nine-year-old girls move step by step down the familiar hall.

"Let's go see the playground," one suggests.

---

* H. Marshall McLuhan, Director, Center for Culture and Technology, University of Toronto, in letter to R.C. Orem, 1966.

"Let's."

They move through the door and down the ramp. A skim down the high slide, accomplished with a degree of abandon, hastily deposits them at the feet of the heavy-springed jumping horses, which they reach out to touch before mounting.

In their own way, these girls are "seeing" the playground. For this is homecoming day at the Blind Children's Center, Los Angeles, California, where students are taught to compensate for lack of vision by using other senses.

The school was founded in 1938 by the Delta Gamma Alumnae of Southern California when lack of care for preschool blind was brought to their attention by Dr. Lillian Ray Titcomb. Knowing the importance of training from the time blindness is diagnosed and before repeated frustrations undermine the child's confidence, she prevailed upon her sorority sisters to sponsor the project.

Today, the school—housed in a modern stucco residence-type building especially designed and built for care of preschool blind—has twenty resident day students and about the same number of "Cradle Club" babies. The babies are given a physical examination at least once a month; their parents also are given special guidance, an important part of the program.

James E. Moxom, who formerly served as executive director of the school, organized, administered, and supervised the program for emotionally disturbed blind children.

Blind himself since age fourteen, Moxom has a deep understanding of these children's needs. He gathered a professional staff of child psychiatrists, child psychologists, and pediatricians. Federico Vaquer, director of the Department of Children's Training and former principal of the Montessori School in Pasadena, has helped install at the school the Montessori method of teaching, a method that instructs through the experience of doing.

"Simply stated, it is a system of doing things that relate to life," Moxom explains. "For instance, a blind child may describe a can opener accurately. Put one in his hands and he has no idea what it is. In the Montessori method, the child learns how to use a can opener. After that, he can certainly describe it.

"Through these methods and with the assistance of the professional staff the school is able to provide a program that will permit sound diagnostic evaluation to determine the child's problems and needs; to provide therapy to meet those needs; to learn more about the problems and how to help through research; and, most important of all, to make it possible for blind children to realize their potential, both for social and vocational living.

There are only two entrance requirements at the Center. The child must be blind or near-blind and he must be under six years of age.

The school day begins with a music session around the piano. What the children lack in harmony, they more than make up in hand-clapping, foot-stamping enthusiasm. They play "accompaniment" on horns, xylophones, drums, noisemakers, and toy pianos. One day, for example, a pretty blond girl climbed onto the piano bench and picked out a few off-key notes alongside the teacher-pianist. The teacher hugged her to let her know her participation was appreciated.

When the music changes to march time, the children, with limited assistance, parade around the room. The music then softens to lead them into the slow tempo of a waltz. Quite unnoticed amidst the fun has been a large measure of training in coordination.

The children sing "America, the Beautiful"; an eager little boy leads the flag salute; they divide into classes, which are conducted with a teacher-to-students ratio of one to four.

One group hurries toward the playground and sets the swings, tricycles, and merry-go-rounds in noisy motion.

In the occupational-therapy room, soft music is heard above the voices of children. For close supervision, the teacher sits in the curve of a half-moon table. And just as coordination was a guest at the earlier music session, manual dexterity is a visitor here.

Each child feels a scrap of material in a basket and identifies it: "Silk, like my party dress." "Wool, like my coat." "Yarn, like my bedroom slippers." Or, as one boy called out after searching the basket carefully, "Hey! Where's the dotted Swiss?"

Before the student graduates, his inquisitive fingers will learn to explore a book with raised felt designs and with raised dots in the form of small hands—right and left, squares, circles, and triangles of various sizes as well as simple long and short lines.

Among other things, the school's director of children's training, Federico Vaquer, has added equipment involving the manipulation of buckles, laces, zippers, various kinds of locks and hooks. . . . Even the vocabulary builds as the child identifies wide, thin, narrow, slender, short, long, or circular pegs and drops them into the proper hole in accompanying blocks of wood.

Lessons in group participation probably start in community singing. Next, in addition to singing, hands clasp to form "London Bridge." The children take turns guessing the name of a song played on the piano, or in finishing a sentence the teacher starts. At times she hides a ticking clock or a fragrant object for them to find. Or perhaps a child will turn an egg beater. The one who guesses the source of the whirring sound makes the next sound for the others to guess.

Another participation experience is in raising sweet peas. The children soak the seed, prepare the soil, and plant the seed. And one delightful, long-anticipated day they pick the flowers and decorate the school.

The school encourages creativity, too. Three boys, for example, have used their initiative to make up a game in which each, one behind the other, pedals a car to the swings. They play awhile and then drive bumper-to-bumper to the barrels, crawl through, and caravan on to the pool for a swim.

This game usually includes a stop at the playhouse, where furnishings, in child-sized modern, include a divan and chairs, a table, a range, a doll buggy. Finger-painting aprons hang beside the china cupboard. A phone on the table teaches dialing and encourages voice communication from diffident youngsters. Here they often find themselves involved in diversionary play conversations: "I'm the mommy. You're the daddy. And this is the baby."

Trips to the zoo, where the children meet animals, are very popular, as are trips to the park, where they ride the merry-go-round horses.

Holidays are made gay and exciting, too.

Christmas is the high point of celebrations. The children touch the tree and the mysterious ornaments; they smell the delicious odors coming from the kitchen; they listen to the music of the season; and they anticipate the excitement of unwrapping gifts.

But educating blind children is only half the job. Bewildered parents need and receive help.

Too often, parents feel guilty. Perhaps, they think, it was something they did—or failed to do. Unless they are reassured, their frustration soon spills over to the child. So they are encouraged to call the Center any time they need advice.

Frequent staff-parent conferences are held. Here, counseling is given on the handling of the child—when to protect, when to ignore.

The Blind Children's Center is endorsed by the Los Angeles County Social Service Commission, the Children's Hospital, Education Departments of the University of California at Los Angeles and the University of Southern California, and by the Frances Blend School for Handicapped Children of the Los Angeles School System.

Many of the Center's graduates are now in universities preparing for careers as teachers, court reporters, musicians, psychologists. While the rehabilitation of a human being is vastly more important than any other consideration, an inestimable number of tax dollars is saved by helping the blind child to become a contributing member of society rather than a potential lifetime institutional case.

Both benefits result from work done by the Blind Children's Center, where the affectionately competent climate is an essential ingredient in the education of the preschool blind.

EDITH M. DEAN

In an important paper, Dr. Ronald Koegler notes that mental disturbance or retardation in children may not be diagnosed until the child enters school. Even problems of a serious and long-standing nature may be ignored or glossed over until the demands of school require a facing up to them.

Montessori schools function as a diagnostic environment in which special problems of three- to five-year-old children are noticed by the observant teacher. For example, the withdrawn child who does not participate in individual or group activities is revealed, as is the hyperactive child who interferes with other children's work.

The structure and activities of the Montessori environment, unlike many loosely organized traditional nursery schools, provide a framework in which the teacher can readily observe deviant behavior. And by detecting a problem when the child is younger, before he has reached traditional nursery-school age, referral can be made and treatment begun sooner.

Although Dr. Koegler emphasizes the usefulness of the Montessori class as a diagnostic environment, he does not overlook its value as a therapeutic *environment for severely disturbed children. For example, the Montessori environment and sensorial approach can provide childhood schizophrenics and organically brain-damaged youngsters with much-needed ego strengthening. Koegler indicates the importance of special classes where trained teachers can use adapted Montessori techniques for such children.*

"The Montessori Classroom: A Diagnostic Environment." *American Montessori Society Bulletin,* 1965.

THE SYLVAN SCHOOL

The Sylvan School, located on more than 100 acres in Ventura County, California, has a poultry ranch, a bee colony, orchards, calf areas, experiments in hydroponics, and a Christmas tree farm. The programs are varied, and include a very successful Montessori nursery for preschoolers of normal intelligence, a special program for retarded and neurologically handicapped youngsters, and a Head Start operation.

Arthur Campbell, educational coordinator for all programs, has noted a definite correlation between the Montessori system and improved educational responses from the retardates. The stimulating, yet structured environment contributes to this improvement. Aids to motivate the child of shorter attention span are being developed and added to the standard repertoire of Montessori didactic materials. For example, a boy who loads ten small autos onto an auto-transport truck and then wheels it to a destination on the other side of the room learns the relationships inherent in the one-to-ten beads, etc. He also has more fun while doing this, which helps increase his attention span.

Since many of the Montessori materials are designed to lead the learner to *future* abstractions on a rather intellectual plane that the retardate may never reach, care is taken to offer the child plenty of material that can be absorbed in the *present*. Music and rhythm are offered in conjunction with counting and language exercises. For example, the song "One Little, Two Little, Three Little Indians" is very effective.

Of course, regular use of the Montessori geometric two- and three-dimensional shapes is meaningful, as is experience with the geographic puzzles, name cards, color gradations, tactile exercise, etc., all of which contain virtually unlimited possibilities for the learning process. Bert Campbell directs the Montessori aspects of the Sylvan programs.

The Sylvan staff members are developing ingenious training aids for such subjects as geography. For example, three-dimensional land forms in pans combine geography, vocabulary, and Montessori "practical life" manual dexterity. When a child pours water into one of these pans he is learning about "harbors," "inlets," "islands," etc., as well as how to pour liquids.

There is a residential facility for special children, who participate in manufacturing equipment and sales projects to gain vocational skills.

One of the authors (Theodore F. Naumann) became very much impressed in this respect when he revisited the Montessori children's house in Frankfurt/Main, Germany, in the summer of 1963. About thirty children, ages two-and-a-half to seven years, were happily learning within the same classroom for several hours each forenoon.

There were no discipline problems or boredom. Gifted, normal, and retarded children were in this group, and each child was learning at his own level and speed, utilizing various types of learning materials. Similar observations were made elsewhere in Europe.

Theodore F. Naumann, and Bobbie N. Parson, "A Creative Learning Environment for Normal and Handicapped Pupils." *The American Montessori Society Bulletin*, Vol. 3, No. 2, 1965.

THE VIA MARSI MONTESSORI SCHOOL

According to Jon Osterkorn, MSW, Executive Director of the Via Marsi Montessori School (Milwaukee), the Via Marsi Society was formed in the fall of 1967 after two years of planning by a group of professionals interested in the application of the Montessori approach to the education of the mentally handicapped and the economically and socially disadvantaged child. The society is under the direction of a professional board of directors elected from the general membership. Board members are generally individuals directly concerned with the educational problems of the handicapped, and come from the fields of medicine, law, social work, education, and labor. The society has three basic areas of interest in regard to Montessori. First, the society, as a nonprofit educational organization, is interested in direct service programs to handicapped and disadvantaged children using the Montessori approach. Second, the society is concerned with research into the cognitive development of handicapped children, and how this development relates to the Montessori classroom environment. Third, the society is interested in the publication of material on the historical development of the Montessori method and movement, and on the application of Montessori techniques with the handicapped. At the present time, the society is directly involved in all of the above areas.

In regard to the direct service programs, the Via Marsi Society sponsors the Via Marsi Montessori School. This program serves twenty children of mixed mental and chronological ages. Both normal and mentally handicapped children work together in integrated classes. All children are between the ages of two-and-one-half and seven years. According to the classification system of the American Association on Mental Deficiency, both the moderate and mild forms of organic mental deficiency are included in the range of children in the program, thus producing an IQ range from 35 to normal within the population of the school. The school is financially supported through a special state and county governmental program that offers 40 percent funds toward the operating budget. The Via Marsi Montessori School also is supported financially by the local Milwaukee chapter of the National Foundation-March of Dimes, for work with children who present Down's Syndrome. All fees are based on the parents' ability to pay, and ten full scholarships are available and in use for children from disadvantaged homes. The school is affiliated with Milwaukee Children's Hospital for diagnostic purposes, and works closely with the staff of the hospital's Special Development Clinic.

All children, both normal and handicapped, are given extensive psychological workups before entering the program, and on an ongoing basis throughout the year. Thirty-day professional treatment reviews and staffings are held with the physician, social worker, psychologists, and teachers on all handicapped children in the program. Two special parent programs are in operation, one for parents of the organically mentally handicapped, and another for parents of normal children from disadvantaged homes. Both programs, along with individual casework services, are under the direction of the school social worker. Plans are under way for a special homebound program to be developed for children unable to participate in the regular five-day-per-week classroom program. It is hoped that this program will take the form of an early stimulation program for young functionally retarded children from the inner-city area that surrounds the school.

In regard to the Via Marsi Society's concern with research, two projects are presently in operation. The first involves an evaluation of the growth and development of the mentally handicapped children in the Via Marsi Montessori School as compared with a matched set of children attending a standard nursery program for mentally retarded children. The research design uses a wide range of standardized tests, along with some specially constructed items to test the development of reasoning abilities. This project will be a two-year study, and a report will be formally issued in the summer of 1970 on the total program. The second research project involves the relationship between the developmental theories of Jean Piaget and cognitive development in the mentally retarded. This project will involve older mentally handicapped children from St. Coletta's School in Jefferson, Wisconsin, and will be conducted in cooperation with the University of Wisconsin–Milwaukee School of Social Welfare and the Via Marsi Society. Several of Piaget's experiments in conservation of substance and length and logical operations will be given to a large number of mentally handicapped children in order to ascertain the relationship between Piaget's stages of cognitive development and the measured language abilities of the children. A report on this project will also be issued and circulated in the late spring of 1969.

The third area of interest for the society is the publication of materials related to the history and growth of the Montessori movement, and the use of Montessori techniques with the mentally handicapped. The Via Marsi Society is an institutional member of the Association Montessori Internationale (Dr. Maria Montessori, Founder and President, 1929–1952).

ANNOTATED BIBLIOGRAPHY WITH EMPHASIS UPON MONTESSORI AND SPECIAL EDUCATION

Ayrault, Evelyn, "The Montessori Method Applied to the Physically Handicapped Child." Mimeographed paper.

The author, a New York State certified psychologist, points out that the Montessori prepared environment helps the handicapped child develop at his own rate of speed according to his innate capacities, in a noncompetitive atmosphere.

The organization, group activities, ground rules, and absorbing individual work of the prepared environment help the handicapped child to gain some mastery of his environment and become a functioning member of the social unit.

Greger, Elsa N., "Favorable Experiences With the Montessori Method Applied to Mental Retardates." Newsletter of the Montessori Foundation of Minnesota, Fall, 1967.

The author describes her experiences in teaching a class of twelve severely retarded youngsters, aged four to eight, at the Washington Boulevard School for multiple-handicapped children in Los Angeles.

The Montessori material was a great help in keeping the children occupied individually according to their capacities and in utilizing the children's "sensitive periods" for acquiring particular learnings.

————, "Occupational Therapy and Current Educational Trends." *The Montessori Magazine.* Vol. 2, No. 4, 1948, pp. 225–234.

The author describes the purposes of occupational therapy for individuals of various ages and conditions. She points out that the Montessori method, which aims to develop fully the capacities of the young child, is a process of active self-education. Montessori principles have implications for occupational therapy with individuals who have mental or physical problems; but, even more importantly, Montessori principles can effectively guide the active self-education of normal individuals, especially the very young.

Kramer, Rita, "Some Children Are Special." *New York Times Magazine,* November 5, 1967.

Half the article is about Vicky Solomonson, retarded granddaughter of Vice President and Mrs. Hubert Humphrey; the other half covers the improving outlook for such children, in terms of new legislation, expanding programs, and public acceptance.

As noted in *This Week* magazine (October 13, 1968), for regular schooling Vicky "attends the Louise Whitbeck Fraser School in Minneapolis, where the Montessori method of teaching is employed to help each retarded child develop at his or her rate."

Naumann, Theodore, and Bobbie Parson, "A Creative Learning Environment for Normal and Handicapped Pupils." *The American Montessori Society Bulletin.* Vol. 3, No. 2, 1965.

The authors describe the initial findings, which are positive, for a demonstration project designed to investigate the question "Can moderately retarded and normal children in modern America effectively learn together?" Say the authors:

The general and specific results may well give impetus to a reconsideration and possibly a restructuring of our special and regular education approaches. The teacher's role, and therefore her training, appears especially . . . in need of certain changes.

Richardson, Sylvia, "A Pediatrician Looks at Montessori for Neurologically Impaired Children." *The American Montessori Society Bulletin*, Vol. 4, No. 4, 1966.

Address given at the 1965 Annual Convention of the National Association for Crippled Children and Adults pointing out the value of the Montessori materials and techniques for the child who has a learning disability. Dr. Richardson stresses that these techniques are very much in line with a "neuro-physiological approach" to learning.

Sister Aquinas Young, O.S.U. "A Critical Analysis of Two Forms of Auto-Education: The Montessori Method and Programmed Instruction." Master of Arts Dissertation submitted to Faculty of Graduate School of Education of the Catholic University of America, March, 1967.

An analysis of the Montessori and programmed instruction approaches to autoeducation in terms of the nature of the child, the learning process, and the role of the teacher.

"The Montessori School in Children's Convalescent Hospital, 1965–1966." Report.

In addition to individual child development resulting from Montessori classes, the presence of the Montessori school has positively affected this (Washington, D.C.) hospital milieu. The group workers, group mothers, nurses, and other hospital staff members borrow ideas and techniques from the Montessori school.

A BIBLIOGRAPHY ON CHILDREN FOR PARENTS, FOCUSING UPON SPECIAL CHILDREN

Abraham, Willard, *Barbara: A Prologue*. New York, Rinehart, 1958.

Ayrault, Evelyn, *You Can Raise Your Handicapped Child*. New York, Putnam's, 1964.

Baruch, Dorothy, *One Little Boy*. New York, Julian Press, 1952.

Bauer, E. Charles, *Retarded Children Are People*. Milwaukee, Bruce Publishing Co., 1964.

Bowers, Joan, *Exceptional Children in Home, School, and Community*. Toronto, J.M. Dent and Sons, 1960.

Buck, Pearl, *The Child Who Never Grew*. New York, John Day, 1950.

Capa, Cornell, and Pines, Maya, *Retarded Children Can Be Helped*. Great Neck, N.Y., Channel Press, 1957.

Chamberlain, Naomi, and Moss, Dorothy, *The Three R's for the Retarded*. New York, National Association for Retarded Children, 1962.

Dittman, Laura, *The Mentally Retarded Child at Home*. Washington, D.C., U.S. Department of Health, Education and Welfare, 1959.

Frank, Mary and Lawrence, *Your Adolescent at Home and in School*. New York, Viking Press, 1956.

French, Edward, and Scott, Clifford, *Child in the Shadows: A Manual for Parents of Retarded Children*. Philadelphia, Lippincott, 1960.

Gallagher, James, *Emotional Problems of Adolescents*. New York, Oxford University Press, 1958.

Getz, Steven, and Rees, Elizabeth, *The Mentally Ill Child: A Guide for Parents*. Springfield, Ill., Charles C. Thomas, 1957.

Gibbs, Frederic Andrews, and Stamps, Frederick, *Epilepsy Handbook*. Springfield, Ill., Charles C. Thomas, 1958.

Halpern, Howard, *A Parents' Guide to Child Pschotherapy*. New York, A.S. Barnes, 1963.

Hood, Oreste, *Your Child or Mine: The Brain-Injured Child and His Hope*. New York, Harper, 1957.

Johnson, Wendell, *Stuttering and What You Can Do About It*. Minneapolis, University of Minnesota Press, 1961.

Kastein, Shulamith, and Trace, Barbara, *The Birth of Language*. Springfield, Ill., Charles C. Thomas, 1966.

Katz, Alfred, *Parents of the Handicapped*. Springfield, Ill., Charles C. Thomas, 1961.

Kirk, Samuel, Karnes, Merle, and Kirk, Winifred, *You and Your Retarded Child: A Manual for Parents of Retarded Children*. New York, Macmillan, 1956.

Levinson, Abraham, *The Mentally Retarded Child: A Guide for Parents*. New York, John Day, 1965.

Lewis, Richard, Strauss, Alfred, and Lehtinen, Laura, *The Other Child— The Brain Injured Child*. New York, Grune & Stratton, 1960.

Lunt, Carroll, *How to Live with Epilepsy*. New York, Twayne Publishers, 1961.

Livingston, Samuel, *Living with Epileptic Seizures*. Springfield, Ill., Charles C. Thomas, 1963.

Martmer, Edgar, ed., *The Child with a Handicap*. Springfield, Ill., Charles C. Thomas, 1959.

Murray, Dorothy, *This Is Stevie's Story*. New York, National Association for Retarded Children, 1966.

Palmer, Charles, *Speech and Hearing Problems: A Guide for Teachers and Parents*. Springfield, Ill., Charles C. Thomas, 1961.

Rogers, Dale, *Angel Unaware*. Westwood, N.J., Fleming H. Revell, 1953.

Rubin, Theodore, *Jordi*. New York, Ballantine, 1962.

———, *Lisa and David*. New York, Ballantine, 1961.

Schreiber, Flora, *Your Child's Speech: A Practical Guide for Parents*. New York, Putnam's, 1956.

Slaughter, Stella, *The Mentally Retarded Child and His Parent*. New York, Harper, 1960.

Strang, Ruth, *Helping Your Child Develop His Potentialities*. New York, Dutton, 1965.

Theodore, Sr. Mary. *The Challenge of the Retarded Child*. Milwaukee, Bruce Publishing Co., 1963.

Woolson, Arthur, *Good-by, My Son*. New York, Harper, 1960.

SELECTED DIRECTORIES

Directory of Residential Schools for the Mentally Retarded. American Association of Mental Deficiency, Willimantic, Conn., 1965.

Directory of Resources for Mentally Ill Children in the United States. The National Association for Mental Health, New York.

Directory of Sheltered Workshops Serving the Mentally Retarded. National Association for Retarded Children, 420 Lexington Avenue, New York, N.Y. 10017.

Directory for Exceptional Children: Schools, Services, Other Facilities. Porter Sargent, 11 Beacon Street, Boston, Mass.

Directory of Camps for the Handicapped. American Camping Association, Bradford Woods, Martinsville, Indiana.

Directory of Catholic Facilities for Exceptional Children in the United States. The National Catholic Education Association, 1785 Massachusetts Ave., N.W., Washington, D.C. 20016.

Guide to Summer Camps and Summer Schools. Porter Sargent, 11 Beacon Street, Boston, Mass.

School Directory Listing (including over 100 Montessori Schools) in *Children's House*, P.O. Box 111, Caldwell, N.J. 07006.

SOME OTHER SOURCES OF INFORMATION

American Speech and Hearing Association. 1001 Connecticut Ave., N.W., Washington, D.C. 20036.

Children's Bureau. U.S. Department of Health, Education and Welfare, Washington, D.C. Publishes "Selected Reading Suggestions for Parents of Mentally Retarded Children," and *Children*, a bi-monthly journal.

Council for Exceptional Children. 1201 16th St., Washington, D.C. Publishes *Exceptional Children*.

International Council for Exceptional Children. NEA, 1210 16th St., N.W., Washington, D.C., 20006.

League for Emotionally Disturbed Children. 171 Madison Ave., New York, N.Y. 10017.

National Association for Mental Health. 10 Columbus Circle, New York, N.Y. 10019.

National Association for Retarded Children. 420 Lexington Avenue, New York, N.Y. 10017. The national organization for parents of retarded children; publishes "Windows of Understanding," a reading list for parents; also a "Selected Bibliography on Religion for the Retarded" including Protestant, Jewish, and Catholic religions, and *Children Limited*, a bi-monthly newspaper.

National Society for Crippled Children and Adults. 2023 West Ogden Ave., Chicago, Ill., 60612. Publishes the journal *Rehabilitation Literature*.

V

Montessori, Research, and the Future

INSIGHTS

1. The concentration required to "complete a cycle of activity"—to follow a task through from start to finish—helps develop self-discipline and self-reliance.

2. The young child has a unique mentality—an absorptive intelligence; and he is guided by laws of learning that differ from those of the older learner.

3. The young learner needs sufficient structure, which the materials and activities of prepared environment provide, but he also requires the concomitant freedom to exercise his self-choice and inner motivation.

4. An orderly environment offers security and encourages "habits of order."

5. Childhood is the sensitive period—the optimum time—for language learning; the child will learn several languages if adequately exposed to them.

6. A basic dimension of the Montessori method is careful attention to the systematic development of the child's listening, speaking, reading, and writing competencies.

7. There are many Montessori exercises designed to help the child master the vocabulary for logical thinking.

8. The Montessori mathematical material offers the child a multisensory approach to learning mathematics; abstract principles are learned inductively with the concrete, manipulatable materials.

9. Montessori's curriculum evolved from her study of what children responded to at various ages. For example, she found that children from three to six are "word lovers" who enjoy learning scientific words and playing grammar games.

10. The array of didactic materials enables each child, in effect,

to follow his own schedule within the framework of a flexible program for the class at large.

11. The child's individual freedom is not limitless; it is bounded by the rights of the group—the "collective interest."

12. An age range of, say, three years in the classroom offers a number of advantages; for example, the younger children can often learn by watching their older colleagues.

One of the most important chapters in the important book A Teaching Method for Brain-injured and Hyperactive Children (*Cruickshank, Bentzen, Ratzeburg and Tannhauser, Syracuse University Press, 1961*) *is Chapter V, "The Teaching Method." The authors note that much of the Montessori method appears to be appropriate for work with hyperactive or brain-injured children, and "many of the teaching suggestions contained in the present chapter are modifications of those of Montessori" (p. 130).*

Perhaps the most important piece of Montessori research with preschool brain-damaged children was that by Dr. William Argy, reported in Rehabilitation Literature *for October, 1965, official journal of the National Society for Crippled Children and Adults, and appearing here in edited form, with permission.*

MONTESSORI VERSUS ORTHODOX: A STUDY TO DETERMINE THE RELATIVE IMPROVEMENT OF THE PRESCHOOL CHILD WITH BRAIN DAMAGE TRAINED BY ONE OF THE TWO METHODS

The possibilities for research on the Montessori method are extensive. To elicit the interest of psychologists in such endeavors and to elicit their cooperation in explorations of child development will expose the educator to the anxieties of putting convictions to the test and of being forced to modify some cherished conceptions. To do so, how-ever, may clarify the psychological implications of educational methods in a way profitable to psychologists as well as educators.*

PREFACES TO ORIGINAL ARTICLE

... This is a very excellent presentation because of several factors: First, the staff of teachers, therapists, psychologists, and coordinator have had a great deal of experience, and this is very important in writing such a particular comparison. It certainly does go to prove that the Montessori method has very definite value in the field of the physically handicapped or in children with brain damage without physical handicap. Second, it proves that there are different kinds of problems and that the orthodox method is more effective in certain types and the Montessori method in others.

Altogether, I feel this is a very necessary contribution and should be read by all those working in education by various methods.

WINTHROP M. PHELPS, M.D.
Medical Director, Children's Rehabilita-tion Institute for Cerebral Palsy, Baltimore

*   *   *   *   *

If there is any single area in working with children's problems in which we are having an actual increase in both numbers and percent-ages, it is the child with mild to moderate brain damage. With better obstetrics and better pediatrics, we save more babies with some degree of cerebral dysfunction. It then must become the responsibility of our helping professions and community agencies to deal in remedial ways with these handicapped children.

Fortunately, as developmental neurology and psychology become more firmly rooted in our clinical settings, we are increasingly able to diagnose and define the types of disturbances in function we are dealing with. Unfortunately our remedial techniques have not kept pace with our ability to diagnose brain damage.

* Dr. Riley W. Gardner, "A Psychologist Looks at Montessori." *The Element-ary School Journal*, Vol. 67, No. 2, November, 1966, p. 82.

Dr. Argy and his colleagues at the District of Columbia Society for Crippled Children have done the field a considerable service in this study, which begins to put in place a current dilemma facing the remedial services, the differential values of current teaching philosophies and methods for the training of brain-damaged children. Dr. Argy clarifies these problems for both his patients and their teachers!

REGINALD S. LOURIE, M.D.
Director, Department of Psychiatry, Children's Hospital of the District of Columbia

INTRODUCTION

For many years the District of Columbia Society for Crippled Children has been training these children by recognized preschool teaching methods adapted to the needs of the child with brain damage. This was augmented by psychological evaluations and speech, occupational, and physical therapies. The results of treatment have been satisfactory. With the rebirth in the United States of the educational philosophy of Dr. Maria Montessori, we became interested in her methods.[1,2] Dr. Montessori accented individualization. Her recognition that sensory organization is dependent on the timing of cortical maturation and her method of directing activities of the child in a group situation seemed to offer an ideal method of correcting the defects that brain-damaged children present.

THE STAFF

The clinical staff consisted of two internationally known orthopedic surgeons whose particular field was cerebral palsy, and neurologists, psychiatrists, pediatricians, otolaryngologists, ophthalmologists, psychologists, and dentists, all of whom were members of their respective specialty boards. Neuroanatomists, pharmacologists, educators, and speech pathologists were called upon for consultations when needed.

The resident staff were teachers, Montessori directresses, therapists, psychologists, and the coordinator. The two orthodox teachers were trained in the education of the preschool child. Their postgraduate experience amounted to six and ten years. The Montessori direct-resses, who had had three and seven years' experience with children with cerebral palsy, were trained in the psychology of the preschool child. They were selected because of their enthusiasm for the project and their excellent rapport with children. They were enrolled in the Whitby School in Connecticut to receive certificates as Montessori directresses. Their activities during this study were under the supervision of the director of the Montessori Institute of Washington, D.C., who has had twenty-five years' experience in conducting Montessori classes and directing classes for Montessori trainees.

There were two speech, two occupational, and two physical therapists, all of whom had had many years' experience in training the child with cerebral palsy and also with our method of men-suration. The senior psychologist had had fifteen years' experience in examining this type of child. The coordinator has been connected with our organization for twelve years.

These well-trained teachers and therapists all conformed to the qualifications of a good teacher.[3] They had rapport with the children, were skilled in the observation of behavior, and were acquainted with each child, aware of his personality and organic handicap. They were capable of recognizing failure and devising methods of cor-rection and, if frustrated in this effort, they were sufficiently well disciplined to seek consultation.

METHODS OF GROUPING

The study was conducted during the 1962–1963 and 1963–1964 school years. Seventy-one children were selected for the study. These children were divided into two classes, Montessori and orthodox. The orthodox classes were designated as controls. There were forty children in the Montessori classes and thirty-one in the orthodox classes. Each class was subdivided into subclasses so that there were two Montessori and two orthodox classes. To each of the four classes a teacher was assigned, each teacher being trained in her specific field.

The children were matched into Groups A, B, and C according to three categories: Chronological Age; Paired Intelligence Quotient; and Computed Beginning Mental Age. Means of the groups were as follows:

		Montessori Classes	Orthodox Classes
Group A:	Mean Beginning CA	54.12 months	56.90 months
Group B:	Mean IQ	95.06	96.06
Group C:	Mean Beginning MA	45.85 months	45.41 months

In Group A were forty Montessori class children and thirty-one orthodox class children; Group B, sixteen each; and Group C, eighteen each. The matching of Groups B and C was made after the completion of the study.

DIAGNOSES

The diagnoses (Table 1) presented considerable variation. All but four children had symptoms that could be definitely related to brain damage. In many there were behavioral, perceptual, and sensory-receptual complications, but because of the scatter of diagnoses it did not seem to be practical to consider them at this time. It is hoped, however, that these variants and their relation to improvement will be studied with the accumulation of a larger number of cases.

METHODS OF EVALUATION

All children received an initial examination by the medical director. Consultations were held with the proper specialist when necessary, and follow-up studies were made frequently. Every child received psychometric evaluation. Detailed records of the history, the objective signs, and the recommendations for treatment were available to the teachers and therapists.

Measurements of progress in months were made on every child at the beginning and the end of the study. The teachers' measurements were oriented toward social maturity and achievement; the speech

TABLE 1.—*Distribution of Diagnoses in Matched Groups*

	Matched Intelligence Quotient		Matched Beginning CA in months		Matched Beginning MA in months	
	M	O	M	O	M	O
Spastic						
Hemiplegia Right	2	2	2	2	—	1
Hemiplegia Left	—	—	3	1	2	1
Paraplegia	1	2	4	4	—	2
Quadriplegia	5	1	7	5	4	4
Athetosis	3	3	4	4	3	2
Rigidity	3	—	6	—	—	1
Flaccidity	—	1	—	1	—	—
Ataxia	—	1	1	3	2	1
Dysarthria	—	4	1	8	5	—
Muscular Dystrophy	—	1	—	1	1	—
Congenital Hypoplasia	—	—	1	—	—	—
Emotional Brain Syndrome	1	1	4	1	—	2
Brachial Palsy	—	—	1	—	—	—
Mongolism	1	—	4	—	—	2
Mixed Dominance	—	—	1	—	—	1
Möbius Syndrome	—	—	1	—	—	—
Phocomelia	—	—	—	1	1	1
TOTAL	16	16	40	31	18	18

CA = Chronological Age   M = Montessori
MA = Mental Age   O = Orthodox

therapists' toward enunciation, pronunciation, and language formation; the physical therapists' measurements toward balance and ambulation; and the occupational therapists' toward hand skills. Each teacher measured her own pupils. The therapists measured children from both classes.

The objectivity of the measurements of these children was assured by the experience, self-discipline, and integrity of the teachers and therapists. This was augmented by the neutrality of the therapists, who measured the children from both classes. Furthermore, there was frequent evaluation by the clinical staff, the psychologist, and the coordinator. Discussions at frequent staff conferences, attended by all members of the resident staff, entered into the attempt to eliminate any tendency toward bias.

TEACHING

The teaching program for the orthodox classes was directed mainly toward the motivation of each child to participate according to his ability in three-, four-, and five-year-old mental activities. There were group activities in a circle: the reading circle, the music circle, and the circle for the projection of lantern slides with comments by the teacher. When circles were used, all of the children received instructions at the same level, directed toward the group. This was supplemented with table work, each child receiving individual attention.

In the Montessori classes, each child worked individually at a different level. In substance, each child developed himself individually in a group situation under the direction of the teacher. Selection of a specific activity was timed with his maturational capabilities.

The differences between the two methods were, first, a matter of equipment. Secondly, the children in the orthodox classes were taught as a group and essentially on the same level, while the children in the Montessori classes, under direction, trained themselves at their specific levels in a group, absorbing, however, by association the knowledge being obtained by their colleagues.

The children left the classrooms individually for therapeutic sessions, administered as frequently as necessary—the number of sessions being prescribed by the consultants.

Direct intrastaff communication took place in formal staff conferences and one-to-one discussions. Indirect communication was effected through the coordinator and the medical director. Thereby the intramural exchange of knowledge and ideas was constant. All members of the resident staff attended the major clinics, and individual members attended the special consultation clinics whenever a problem involving a child related to the members' particular discipline.

Our facility being a day school, with no formal transportation facilities, there was a continuing daily contact between the members of the staff and at least one adult member of the family constellation. More formal conferences were also held with the individual parents, usually conducted by the psychologist, the coordinator, or the medical director. At times some other member of the staff conducted these conferences when that member and the particular parent had a more wholesome rapport.

The study indicated that in all three groups (Matched Mean Chronological Age [see, for example, Figure 1], Paired Matched Intelligence Quotient, and Matched Beginning Mental Age) the improvement was greater in the Montessori class than in the orthodox. The significant improvement, where it existed, would indicate that the improvement observed would be reproducible in others. The marked changes in the Developmental Quotients would indicate improvement rather than growth. It is interesting to note that the most striking improvement in the Montessori class occurred in those variables that are principally involved as the medium language formulation and expression (see Figure 2).

The results obtained are primarily indications of achievement. Alertness, responsiveness, interest in surroundings, and powers of concentration[4] are mainly reflected by those achievements in the school situation although they have also been confirmed by our own observations. These observations, of course, apply to both groups.

The mean improvement of the Montessori classes showed an improvement of the whole profile. This was the purpose of our study: to find a method that would more adequately develop the whole child. By the procedures used in matching, measuring, and analyzing in this study, the Montessori method seemed to prove that we accomplished this objective.

The results are interesting but should not be considered as conclusive. They are not sufficiently outstanding to issue a mandate for a revolution in the methods of training these children. The most we can say, at this time, is that these results are provocative and warrant more intensive and extensive study.

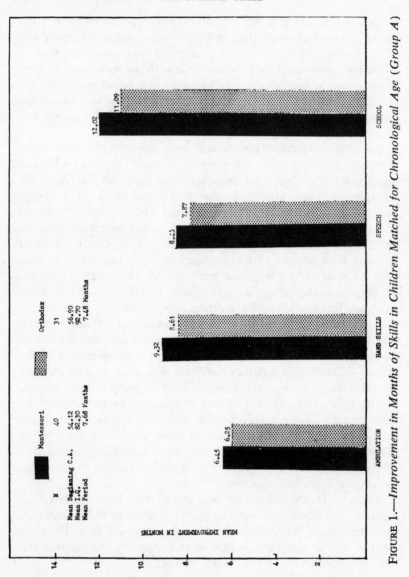

FIGURE 1.—*Improvement in Months of Skills in Children Matched for Chronological Age (Group A)*

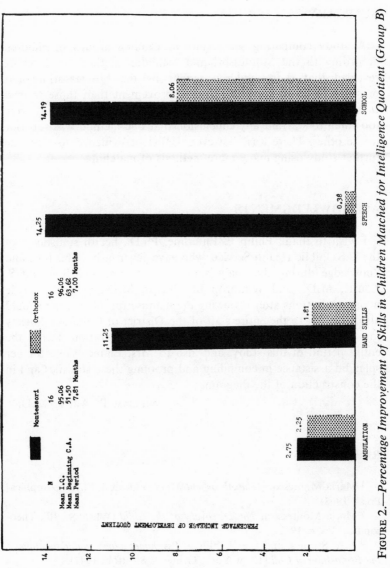

FIGURE 2.—*Percentage Improvement of Skills in Children Matched for Intelligence Quotient (Group B)*

SUMMARY

A study comparing the results of training groups of children according to the Montessori and orthodox methods of teaching revealed that those children taught by the Montessori method presented a more comprehensive improvement than those trained by the orthodox method. The numbers involved in the study were too small to warrant any conclusion that one method was superior to the other. There was, however, sufficient evidence to motivate further study using many more methods of matching.

ACKNOWLEDGMENTS

I wish to thank Philip E. Enterline, Ph.D., health statistician of the U.S. Public Health Service, who gave generously of his time and knowledge during the analysis of the statistics, and Reginald S. Lourie, M.D., and Winthrop M. Phelps, M.D., who also made many suggestions after reviewing the manuscript. Due credit should also be given to the entire staff of the District of Columbia Society for Crippled Children for their excellent cooperation during the entire period of this study, and also to Mrs. Elaine Wolfe for her splendid assistance in compiling and proofing these statistics and in the construction of the diagrams.

WILLIAM P. ARGY, M.D.

REFERENCES

[1] Maria Montessori, *The Absorbent Mind* (Wheaton, Ill., Theosophical Press, 1963).

[2] Maria Montessori, *The Discovery of the Child* (Wheaton, Ill., Theosophical Press, 1962).

[3] A.A. Strauss, and L.E. Lehtinen, *Psychopathology and Education of the Brain-Injured Child* (New York, Grune & Stratton, 1947).

[4] R.S. Illingworth, *The Development of the Infant and Young Child, Normal and Abnormal*, 2nd ed. (Edinburgh, E. & S. Livingstone, 1963).

BIBLIOGRAPHICAL READINGS

Abercrombie, M.L.J., *Perceptual and Visuo-motor Disorders in Cerebral Palsy: A Survey of the Literature*. London, The Spastics Society, 1964. (Little Club Clinics in Developmental Medicine, No. 11.)

Cruickshank, W.M., *A Teaching Method for Brain-Injured and Hyperactive Children: A Demonstration-Pilot Study*. Syracuse, N.Y., Syracuse University Press, 1961.

Dekaban, A., *Neurology of Infancy*. Baltimore, Williams & Wilkins, 1959.

Gesell, A., and Amatruda, C.S., *Developmental Diagnosis: Normal and Abnormal Child Development: Clinical Methods and Pediatric Applications*, 2nd ed. New York, (Hoeber) Harper, 1949.

Gesell, A., and Ilg, F.L., *The Child from Five to Ten*. New York, Harper, 1946.

Holt, K.S., "The Criteria Which Must Be Satisfied in the Assessment of the Long Term Results of Treatment," in *Child Neurology and Cerebral Palsy: A Report of an International Study Group, St. Edmund Hall, Oxford, 1960*. London, National Spastics Society, 1961. (Little Club Clinics in Developmental Medicine, No. 2.)

Johnson, M.K., Zuck, F.N., and Wingate, K., "The Motor Age Test: Measurement of Motor Handicaps in Children with Neuromuscular Disorders Such As Cerebral Palsy." *J. Bone and Joint Sur.* July, 1951. 33–A:3:698–707.

Schwartz, R.P., Zuck, F.N., and Johnson, M.K., "The Need and Resources for Stimulating Volition of Children with Cerebral Palsy: and a Report of Progress of Such Children Under In-Patient Circumstances," in Charles N. Pease, ed., *American Academy of Orthopaedic Surgeons Instructional Course Lecture Series*. Vol. IX, pp. 105–118. Ann Arbor, J.W. Edwards, 1952.

Williams, J.M., "The Effect of Emotional Factors on Perception," in *Child Neurology and Cerebral Palsy: A Report of an International Study Group, St. Edmund Hall, Oxford, 1960*. London, National Spastics Society, 1961. (Little Club Clinics in Developmental Medicine, No. 2.)

During the early years of its renaissance in America, the Montessori movement has had to concern itself primarily with survival in the face of a tradition-oriented educational power structure. As the Montessori position becomes more secure and gains are consolidated, the movement can pass into a new phase of "quality control." Because of a demand for Montessori teachers far outstripping the supply, quantity rather than quality considerations have been paramount in the past. In many cases, Montessori teachers have been imported from Europe and the Far East to open schools, and a number of "crash" training courses have been instituted in the United States in response to pressures to produce Montessori teachers. What is now needed is a vigorous program to strengthen standards of recruitment, selection, and training of Montessori personnel. According to Educational Technology *(July 15, 1967):*

A growing demand for nursery-school and kindergarten teachers trained in the Montessori method has prompted Xavier University of Cincinnati to expand its Montessori teacher training program, founded in 1965 and the first in the U.S. at a university. The expansion will be financed by a grant of $174,000 by Carnegie Corporation of New York.

"The program at Xavier is for graduate students," explains Raymond F. McCoy, dean of the graduate school and chairman of the department of education, "and it insists on a broad background of courses in educational psychology, philosophy, research, and administration in addition to the study of the Montessori approach. The Montessori courses are also available to teachers from public and parochial schools who can adapt what they learn to their regular classroom work.

This type of development can only be viewed as encouraging.

Also, it is no secret that the name "Montessori" cannot be copyrighted, and its use by a school, of course, is no assurance of a genuine Montessori operation. Supervision and accreditation of Montessori schools are still limited in scope and effectiveness. In the meantime, many parents, educators, and others have found helpful the "Guide to the Essential Features of a Good Montessori School" in A Montessori Handbook, *edited by R.C. Orem (Putnam's, 1965).*

RESEARCH ON MONTESSORI AND THE DISADVANTAGED

I first had an experience, you might say, with Maria Montessori in Chicago. I was visiting with some academic friends there. This experience has shaped much of what I think about all of Montessori (*e.g.* Montessori, 1917) I have read since and all of the Montessori classrooms I have seen since. Twenty underprivileged Negro children worked quietly there that day on projects they had chosen and the quiet non-intrusive directress spoke quietly to each child individually. I felt that there was intensity of experience there, interest, involvement, and a burgeoning autonomy. The Dean of the Graduate School, who accompanied us, was a child psychologist. He had never seen such an impressive sight, and he had seen many a pre-school classroom before. Discipline, order, quiet, interest. Now a number of Montessori observational experiences have suggested something else to me. Each Montessori classroom varies in content and style, but there seems to be a particular philosophy and spirit which transcends these local features, whether it be Chicago, Denver, or Cincinnati, and whether the classroom be quiet or active, outdoors or indoors, in groups or alone. That spirit is autonomy via interesting projects for the child growing into an adult through the education in his childhood.*

The Cincinnati Autonomy Test Battery (CATB) has been designed to study autonomous growth and development of young children. In this test battery, the word "autonomy" refers to *self-regulating behaviors that facilitate effective problem solving*. The autonomous child is a good problem solver. He shows *curiosity* about problems, he can *innovate* alternative solutions, and he has good ability to *analyze* problems into their parts. It is rare to find all these tendencies and abilities in just one child.

Each child has his personal strengths, and early childhood

* Thomas J. Banta, "Educating Children for Adulthood." *Young Children*, Vol. 21, No. 5, May, 1966.

education must capitalize on these while aiding the child in developing further his problem-solving strategies. Educational programs that aspire to more than conventional answers to conventional problems must somehow take into account the child's capacity and interest in novel problems and novel solutions. Intelligence must come to be regarded as something more than conventional, quick, and appropriate answers to standardized questions. This is where the CATB comes in. With the CATB, we are tracking down the ways in which early childhood education works, and which kinds of educational practice are most effective.

One educational practice, Montessori, has attracted our attention in relation to work with the disadvantaged. It has become clear, however, that Montessori does not constitute a single approach to children that is the same the world over, or even throughout this country. In fact, within Cincinnati, where we have studied several Montessori programs, great differences among teachers and teacher-child relationships have been observed. It turns out that even where a teacher has been trained in Montessori education and is certified and evaluated by the Montessori Society, Montessori enthusiasts themselves raise questions as to whether some classrooms are "really" Montessori at all. I have discussed this question more fully in a paper, "Is There Really a Montessori Method?"

The most important aspect of classrooms we have studied divides them along a scale from highly structured to highly permissive. When you open the door of a highly structured classroom, you do not hear much noise; children are seated quietly working with didactic materials; group activities are limited; children are highly organized and controlled, sometimes by obvious instructions to children ("Now go over and get something to work with"), and sometimes by subtle directions (a look of disapproval when materials are used improperly). When you walk into a highly permissive classroom you hear many sounds—children singing, or furniture being moved about to construct forts or houses; some children are working by themselves while others are organizing a march or a family; the teacher may be holding a child or leading songs; the teacher is more of a participant than a detached observer; there is much more body contact between teacher and child. The highly structured classroom is task-oriented while the highly permissive classroom is fantasy-oriented and free-play-oriented. Both kinds of classrooms occur within Montessori philosophy and Montessori training because the teacher brings to the teaching situation a whole life history of relationships with children; the resulting teacher personality has a direct bearing on what will happen in the classroom.

The findings discussed below are based upon Cincinnati Montessori classrooms that we have studied closely. Of the three classrooms, one is highly structured, one is less structured, and the third is highly permissive. For comparison with disadvantaged children, the highly structured classroom is a relatively high-tuition school for white middle- and upper-middle class children. The remaining two are sponsored by the Office of Economic Opportunity for predominantly lower-class Negro children. In addition, some comparisons are made with lower-class Negro children who did not attend prekindergarten classes.

Our findings from previous studies show that problem-solving behaviors are more developed in the culturally advantaged groups we have studied, and most poorly developed on the average among the nonprekindergarten lower-class groups, as one might expect. Our purpose, however, was not to demonstrate the obvious, but to study what kinds of gains are greatest and what kinds of gains are lacking, and finally, to find out what these changes or the lack of them should be attributed to. Here are four provisional generalizations about types of classrooms and their different effects on disadvantaged children.

1. *Innovative behavior is lacking among the lower-class children; it can be modified through prekindergarten experience, but the upper-class children have a considerable head start.* In a test that involves a game of "getting the dog to get to his bone" via varying routes, 23 percent of lower-class children found *no* new or novel routes for the dog to get to his bone. *All* upper-class children found at least one novel route and their scores were dramatically higher. Lower-class children tended to confine their behavior to imitations of the demonstration provided by the tester, as though this is the only "safe" way to go. Montessori classrooms showed improvement

over comparison nonprekindergarten children, but it appears that the highly permissive classroom had the greatest effect.

2. *Analytic thinking can be trained in structured prekindergarten classrooms, but again the upper-class child has the advantage.* We test analytic thinking by asking the child to find a picture of an ice cream cone embedded in other, more complex figures. This is somewhat like the games found in a typical Sunday newspaper comic section where the reader is asked to look at the picture of a tree and to find as many outlines of faces as he can in the drawing. Again, it turned out that the Montessori classrooms differed, and here the differences were even more dramatic. This time, however, the greatest improvement was found in the highly structured classroom. Almost no gains were found in the social, expressive, emotion-oriented classroom at the end of the first year. These results go contrary to some theories of the development of analytic thinking, which suggest that such patterns are laid down very early in the child's life and are relatively nonmodifiable. This finding holds out considerable hope for training productive thought processes among the disadvantaged. It appears that structured, controlled classrooms do this best.

3. *Learning processes are greatly improved through prekindergarten experience, and under certain conditions lower-class children do slightly better than upper-class children.* We have developed a test for two kinds of learning. One kind of learning reflects ability to master a task set by an adult for the child; this is called *intentional* learning. Another kind of learning reflects the ability of the child to learn things *other than* those he is told to learn; this is called *incidental* learning, the learning of aspects of the problem incidental to the main task. In *incidental* learning, lower-class children do at least as well as upper-class children and the prekindergarten children do slightly better. In *intentional* learning, the prekindergarten children, whether lower- or upper-class, did much better than children who did not go to school. There appeared to be no important differences between upper- and lower-class children after prekindergarten on this intentional learning task. Whatever the component parts of this complex kind of learning, the prekindergarten experiences greatly

improved the lower-class child, regardless of whether they were highly structured or highly permissive Montessori classrooms.

4. *Highly structured classrooms reduce curiosity motivation and exploratory behavior.* We studied curiosity and exploratory behavior with what we call the "curiosity box." The curiosity box is a wooden box with many gadgets, switches, holes, handles, springs, and shiny attractive materials attached to it. The child can look in the box, can stick his hand inside the box to explore it tactually, and can open up one end of the box which is closed with a latch. The curiosity box is placed in front of each child and the tester says, "Here is something for you to play with." Nothing more is indicated. Most children began to explore the box, gradually becoming more and more interested in what it had in store for them. Upper-class children generally did more exploring, more talking while exploring, and tended to move around more. Lower-class children, by contrast, talked less, explored less, and appeared uninterested.

There are dramatic differences, however, as a result of different kinds of prekindergarten experiences. By far the highest scores obtained by lower-class Negro children were found in the permissive classroom (average score, 21). *The lowest exploratory behavior scores of prekindergarten classrooms we have studied came from the highly structured Montessori children*, and these were middle- to upper-middle class white children from relatively advantaged homes (average score, 10). Two groups of lower-class Negro children who did not go to prekindergarten also showed little curiosity and exploratory behavior (average scores, 8 and 3). The less structured classroom showed curiosity and exploratory behaviors between those of the other more extreme groups (average score, 15).

In summary, we have found that classrooms function on an either-or basis: either analytic thinking *or* curiosity and innovative behaviors are improved. But, at present, we cannot have everything. All classrooms do appear to improve conventional learning processes. It is our hope that we can eventually develop procedures that will produce not only improved conventional learning processes, but produce improvement in analytic thinking *along with* maintenance of curiosity motivation, exploratory behavior, and innovative behavior. At the present time it appears that teaching practices do not improve *all* factors in autonomous problem solving within one classroom. Much needed are educational innovations that would optimize autonomous functioning in all areas.

THOMAS J. BANTA

Although there may be those who prefer to believe that the Montessori method is a closed system, completed and beyond change, the fact of the matter is that Montessori herself many times indicated its incompleteness. She saw in her work only the promising beginnings of a "new education."

Currently, one of the more exciting possibilities for research is the coupling of basic Montessori principles with the emerging educational technology. As George Stevens has noted:

> The Montessori method and didactic apparatus, while excellent in purpose, can be greatly expanded and elaborated within our current understanding of learning theory. And the electronic technology now available to us could revolutionize the materials originally designed by Dr. Montessori.

Dr. Ofiesh and Dr. O'Keefe mention the Greeley, Colorado, project directed by Dr. Glen Nimnicht. In discussion with the editor, Dr. Nimnicht mentioned that the first thing he has his new teachers do is read a copy of The Montessori Method.

THE NEW EDUCATIONAL TECHNOLOGY: POSSIBILITIES AND PROSPECTS FOR EARLY LEARNING

> Her system, her philosophy, and her method have a beautiful symmetry and wholeness that transcend much of the fragmentary nature of current efforts at educational reform. . . . But the important fact

about her contribution is that it leads to a systematized and total educational program for the young child.*

INTRODUCTION

Maria Montessori would probably have championed our newly developing educational technology, for the effective application of modern audiovisual equipment, computers, programmed textbooks, teaching machines, and "talking typewriters" to education implies a "preparing of the environment" compatible with her own philosophy and approach.

Many aspects of the blossoming new technology have received considerable attention by educators, publishers, researchers, and the general public. Publishers have added programmed textbooks to their standard fare, some focusing their entire effort on preparing programmed materials. Because of the great difference in cost between developing a text-programmed course and a computer-programmed course, most of the current effort is going into programmed texts. (The cost for developing one computerized course of instruction ranges from $350,000 to $500,000, and the computer itself may cost $40,000 to $50,000.) According to Dr. LeRoy Aserlind,[1] less than ten years ago 90 percent of all available programmed instruction was machine-oriented and 10 percent textbook oriented, while today the figures are reversed. It should be noted that programmed instructional materials for exceptional children are very scarce. In fact, in an extensive review of the literature, Dr. Aserlind found no computerized programs (computer-assisted instruction) for the exceptional child.

Indeed, computerized programs in general are scarce. It has been said that if, for example, a sixth-grade teacher wished to teach her class for a full year using computer programs, she would be unable to do so, for the curricula do not yet exist. Not only is it expensive to develop a computer-assisted instruction (CAI) program, but such development demands extensive time and effort by highly trained people.

* John Henry Martin, "Montessori After 50 Years." *Teachers College Record*, March, 1965, p. 552.

Of course, extensive efforts are being made to overcome the problems of computer expense and program preparation. The notion of time-sharing, developed at MIT, is under investigation as one means of lessening computer expense. One such example is "Operation Computel," a program developed by the Computation Center of the Illinois Institute of Technology with teletypewriters installed in twenty Chicago city and suburban high schools and junior colleges. These teletypewriters are linked by conventional telephone lines to the institute's data-processing center, and enable 500 students to participate in a program for a cost of only $2,500 for each school during an academic year.[2]

The use of computers for instructional programs is only one of many ways computers can serve education: general business accounting; student accounting; school research, evaluation, and analysis, can all be expedited with computer assistance.

In regard to program development, a field still in its infancy, a number of centers are undertaking to prepare and test various kinds of computer-assisted instructional programs. In many cases these efforts are heavily supported by federal funds. For instance, under the directorship of Dr. Robert Glaser, staff members at the Learning Research and Development Center of the University of Pittsburgh (one of the first R & D centers established by the U.S. Office of Education) are developing curricular materials that can be used for CAI programs. In addition to federal and university efforts, private corporations such as the System Development Corporation are contributing significantly to the development of CAI programs.

As suggested earlier, the scope of educational technology is broad, encompassing concepts that utilize nonautomated, as well as automated equipment. However, in the remainder of this paper, we shall focus on three aspects of the new technology of education: (1) the need for process-oriented educational research and demonstration projects, (2) the notion of the computerized learning center, and (3) the concept of the responsive environment approach—both automated and nonautomated.

INNOVATIONAL EDUCATION SYSTEMS

Need for Process Demonstration

A basic problem in educational research and development in the early learning years is an apparent inability to extrapolate from the learning laboratory and the experimental school in the research institution to the "Living Lab"—*i.e.*, the frontline classroom. Research findings must be translated, where applicable, into classroom practices.

Educational researchers in early learning are beginning to recognize that no educational problems in our society are so imperative as those generated by the socioeconomic conditions of the inner city. These crucial problems will come to dominate the attention of economists, sociologists, and educators for many years. Planners in some seventy cities are this year devising developmental schemes and social projects.

There is real danger that education and training institutions with shiny new façades, but offering the same learning menus that have already failed to meet current needs, will be set down in the middle of these areas. The presence of the most modern bricks and mortar will not solve the educational problems, nor will educational TV or the electronic wizardry of computer-assisted instruction. The critical elements are relevancy of educational content and dynamic application of the expanding science of behavioral development.

The growing capability of educators to structure, in socially relevant form, the behavior of the very young has given us hope that we may soon be able to restructure the asocial character of the older asocial behavior patterns produced by chance, incidental learning, and by environments we are pledged to change. Anachronistic education and training systems must not be set down in the inner-city complexes being planned. All the strength of competent education and training technology must be brought to bear on the demonstration city projects, to ensure that new systems are relevant in content and apply the expanding science of behavioral development to the fullest extent.

A central focus of research and development in education and training technology must be provided. Projects for education and training in demonstration city projects, poverty programs, slum and ghetto projects, or inner-city education systems should be reviewed, integrated, and coordinated where possible, and restructured where necessary, to ensure they are not mere replications of old software in shiny new faces of brick and stone.

As projects proceed and the science of behavioral development grows, an information center with publications, as well as information storage and retrieval capability, must be provided. Presently, the methods and techniques of early education developed by the genius of Maria Montessori and Omar K. Moore; the subsequent research and deliberations of Martin Deutsch, Glen Nimnicht, Lasser Gotkin, and others are reaching only a handful of kindergartens and nurseries, and only a small fraction of the Head Start units.

Out of the very few current and past truly innovative projects, an expanding knowledge of administration and management of innovative and exemplary educational systems for the early learning years is being generated. Some of this knowledge is being recorded as in the case of Responsive Environment Demonstration Projects, presently supported by the Office of Economic Opportunity. There is a need for the development of administrative guides, on-site management consultation, and feasibility study services. There is need to establish centers for demonstrations that will bridge the gap between the early-learning science laboratory and the early-learning centers of society. The "not feasible" of today is often the necessity of tomorrow (witness the electric car). It is not enough to pay lip service to science; the "no" answers are as important as the "yes" answers in mankind's reach for controls over his destiny.

Careful study must be made of the present efforts to establish computerized learning centers, the "talking typewriter," and the responsive environment approach to early learning.

THE COMPUTERIZED LEARNING CENTER

Due to the previously mentioned problems of cost and program preparation, computerized learning centers at present exist mainly in research or demonstration settings.

In the computerized learning environment the student is seated at a console that customarily includes a TV screen or a cathode ray tube (CRT), earphones, typewriter keyboard, microphone, and possibly an electronic pointer, although very recent developments allow children to point to the screen with their fingers and even to use a "talking pencil." CAI can today present to the student an arbitrary sequence of audio messages of any length and any desired sequence of pictures through special random-access audio and video files. When the student depresses the key on the keyboard, appropriate symbols or characters appear on the CRT just as they normally would on a piece of paper in the typewriter.

Pointing techniques are proving useful in the new classroom. In response to a request to point to a particular item on the CRT or TV screen, the student places the pointer, his finger, or pencil against the face of the CRT. After detecting at what part of the picture the student is pointing, the computer provides the student with the next sequence on the screen, which may be a "remedial" sequence if the student has pointed to a "wrong" item, or the next logical sequence if he made a "correct" response.

Any subject that can be taught by a lecture, such as those customarily presented on educational TV, can easily be presented on the CRT. The main characteristic of CAI, however, is its adaptiveness to the idiosyncratic qualities of the learner. In dealing with the exceptional child this adds a most valuable element. The audiovisual teacher system can now enter into a dialogue with every student through questioning the student's assimilation of the verbal or visual stimuli presented. When the student demonstrates mastery of the subject, the computer, noting this, will present the next segment of the course. If the student's response indicates that he has failed to learn the material (either by giving the wrong answer to a question or hesitating too long in making a response), the system will branch him to a different presentation of the same concept. Remedial sequences presented to the student are designed to meet his peculiar deficiency. In contrast to the traditional lesson plan, which is "covered" by the teacher, the student in this case will not be permitted to proceed to more difficult concepts or materials until he has indicated that he has mastered the prerequisites.

CAI combines the advantages of the programmed text and the multimedia teaching machine. Through CAI the child can be presented both verbal and visual information and asked to point either with his finger or the electronic pointer to a particular item on the TV screen. A child can readily be taught to discriminate between the sounds or shapes of various letters; vocabulary can be taught by presenting pictures and sound together.

It is claimed that one of the major results of CAI is the development of the student's auditory and visual discriminatory skills. In the teaching of reading these can include such items as phonics, letter recognition, letter formation, spelling, and number concepts.

Probably the most distinguishing characteristic of CAI is the child's progression through an individually tailored course. In an ideal CAI program every child will travel down his own uniquely optimum path of learning, advancing through the material as fast as he can demonstrate proficiency. Repetitious drill is minimized because the computer can quickly detect and eliminate material that has been learned to a certain predetermined level of performance. Likewise, the child can be gradually eased into the next step because errors on difficult material can be caught as soon as they occur.

Furthermore, a complete record of each student's errors and the time required to learn are available to the teacher or researcher. In addition to indicating the individual's progress, these records provide educational programmers with a powerful tool for rapid evaluation of the course, so that sections of the course may be immediately modified if deemed desirable. Thus, empirical development of instructional materials based on student evidence can become a significant aspect of the computer-assisted learning center.

Since disadvantaged children from poverty backgrounds often lack fundamental perceptual and discriminatory skills, basic language skills, and the sense of achievement, motivation and positive self concept that the middle-class child normally acquires by an early age, the computerized learning center can be especially beneficial.

The following section briefly describes one of the most recent and definitive national demonstrations of the application of educational technology to early learning. This involves the responsive environment process and the Edison Responsive Environment equipment (the "talking typewriter") as applied to disadvantaged children in three projects sponsored by the Community Action Program of the War on Poverty Agency—the Office of Economic Opportunity.

WHAT IS THE RESPONSIVE ENVIRONMENT CONCEPT?

The responsive environment process, which has an affinity for the Montessori approach to education, derives largely from the genius of Dr. Omar K. Moore. The process is explained in considerable detail in his article "*Autotelic Responsive Environments and Exceptional Children.*"[3] Many applications of Moore's concept utilize a "talking typewriter" (Edison Responsive Environment, or ERE) as a major tool, although Dr. Moore himself does not look upon the "talking typewriter" as the most essential or even necessary element of responsive environment. He is as concerned with the nonautomated aspects of the responsive environment approach as with the "automated" factors.

Four stages of procedures have been identified by O.K. Moore for accomplishing his learning objectives through learning to read. According to Moore, the child not only learns to read through autotelic responsive environments, but more importantly, he "learns to learn"—to develop the desire to continue learning, to view learning as exciting in its own right, and, in the process, to develop a healthy self concept and the capacity for flexibility and autonomous behavior!

Further, through Moore's approach, reading is considered inseparable from other areas of the language arts, such as listening, speaking, writing, and spelling, and is treated as an integral aspect of language development.

In the first stage, "Free Exploration," the child literally plays with his new toy, the typewriter, which is usually located in a booth with an attendant nearby to respond to the child when he indicates a need. The typewriter has been programmed so that when a key is depressed it will respond visually (by typing that letter, symbol, or number) and audibly (by the key voice saying the name of the letter, symbol, or number). Through this type of exploring, certain essential learnings vital to the total process of reading are initiated. The child learns, for example, that letters are symbols, and that these symbols have various shapes.

"Free Exploration" activities continue until the child begins to tire of the game. Suddenly, he finds that the keys no longer respond to his touch, and he must discover the rules of a new game.

In the second stage, or game, "Search and Match," the booth attendant places a card programmed with letters into the machine. The child must first press the key matching the one he is shown, and later he must type the key representing the letter he hears. He continues to get visual and auditory reinforcement when he makes a correct response, and discovers that one of the rules of this new game is that only one key, the correct one, will depress. He gradually learns that there are upper- and lower-case letters.

This new game can be quite challenging because programming allows for highly developed skills to be presented in a variety of ways. By the end of the "Search and Match" stage in the learning process, the child can readily identify the vowel and consonant letters of the typewriter with their appropriate letter names and sounds, from either auditory or visual cues, and he can recognize a few sight words.

The third stage, "Word Construction," involves both reading and writing, and the child working through this phase of the learning process is well on his way to reading and the related area of writing. Cards are programmed with stories dictated by an individual child or by a small group of children. Phonetic analysis, structural analysis and comprehension skills are then programmed in game form using these stories as a basis.

The final stage is "Reading and Writing," in which the children are able to read and write on their own. A wide variety of materials together with programmed cards can be used in this phase. Indeed, the greater the varieties of materials used, the more stimulating the adventure of reading becomes.

Throughout the entire process, the child's attendant plays an extremely important and distinct role. He or she must have a basic knowledge of the stages of the process, and sufficient understanding of programming and its relation to reading development. Above all, the attendant must have an awareness and intuitiveness of the child and his abilities, and give assistance only in a positive manner. Like the Montessori directress, the attendant's role is to guide, not to instruct.

In summary, a responsive environment (whether or not it includes a "talking typewriter") must:

· Permit the learner to explore freely.

· Inform the learner immediately of the consequences of his own activities.

· Permit the learner to learn at a rate determined by the learner.

· Permit the learner to make maximum use of his capacity for discovery.

In addition, various relationships facilitate the likelihood that the learner will make numerous interrelated discoveries about his world.

The responsive environment is autotelic, or self-rewarding, and motivation is considered to be intrinsic, rather than based on extrinsic rewards or punishments. Indeed, key words in the entire process are "child-centered" and "self-directed," and, as noted, the attending adult takes a role of guiding rather than directly teaching.

THREE RESPONSIVE ENVIRONMENT PROJECTS

Early in 1966 the Office of Economic Opportunity activated three demonstration projects designed to test in various operational situations the effectiveness of teaching disadvantaged children and adults in a variety of subject areas, through various applications of programmed automated education and the responsive environment process. Each of the three projects served the population in a different geographical area. Each involved a different type of administration: a large public school system, a large welfare department, and the early learning laboratory of a state college. The project participants represented a broad spectrum of the lower-income segment of the population, with pupils from three-and-a-half years of age to adults, and included bilingual students, members of minority groups, truants, and dropouts.

Because of the variables in administration, geographical locations, and the target populations served, the Office of Economic Opportunity (OEO) contracted with the Center for Educational Technology at the Catholic University of America in Washington, D.C., to provide the administrative, advisory, management, and evaluation services needed to coordinate the various components of the three projects and have a continually updated assessment of the progress of each.

The task of the Center for Educational Technology, under the direction of Dr. Gabriel D. Ofiesh, was to view all aspects of the projects objectively and evaluate them without bias. This project-management service assisted OEO in technical surveillance in the form of reviewing qualifications and performance of key personnel, coordinating experimental design, evaluating equipment, curriculum and operational procedures, establishing reporting data requirements, reviewing and analyzing reports from the projects, providing periodic reports to OEO, evaluating each of the three projects by measuring the effects of the program on the target population, recommending follow-up and justification for continuance, and selecting areas suitable for replication of the methods and techniques demonstrated.

Project management, although accepted in industrial and military affairs, has been almost unknown in the field of education. The close surveillance that was exercised by Catholic University's Center for Educational Technology has circumvented many potential problems. Some emotionally charged situations have been resolved quietly, though not easily—others have not. The individual projects have been kept on course in accordance with the primary objectives, and the results are encouraging. The general approach and some of the processes are effective in each of the environments, insofar as preliminary results suggest they are solving the problem of education deprivation more effectively than conventional methods. Managerial and administrative procedures are being documented in order to facilitate replication. The process of training personnel in the application of the techniques has appeared to be effective.

The New York City Project

In New York City, the demonstration is being carried out under the auspices of the New York City Board of Education and is directed by Dr. Edward A. Welling, Jr. Included are children ranging from kindergarteners through elementary and secondary level pupils with substantial environmental handicaps, as well as adult illiterates. The emphasis in New York is largely on the automated aspects of the approach rather than the nonautomated, although there are some nonautomated elements in the overall system. Five-year-olds are typing sentences; some of them are composing and typing their own stories. In the related classroom they are responding appropriately to a cultural configuration that is often absent in their homes.

Parents have been stimulated, and as a result a parents' organization has been formed whose support for early education may have a significant future impact on the educational system.

Potential dropouts and boys and girls with the highest truancy records in their schools are attending these responsive environment classes regularly and apparently with great enthusiasm. They are responding in the talking typewriter booths to a variety of curricular materials, including their own choice of music, sports heroes, and even poetry. Typing stories and answering questions, they are eager to learn what they consider relevant to their own interests.

Progress is being measured against control groups, and programs for future use and dissemination are being prepared by competent educators who understand the methods and procedures of the responsive environment process.

The Chicago Project

In Chicago, the demonstration is called Project Breakthrough and is administratively under the direction of Louis A. Scott and the Department of Public Aid, rather than the school system. This project, about half the size of the New York project, includes 120 preschoolers from some of the most abject poverty-stricken homes in the nation. This project includes extensive application of non-automated as well as automated approaches. Intensified casework is being done with half the families of the experimental students, and regular casework with the other half. A link between project, home, and community has been provided through the hiring of an indigenous neighborhood leader who assists the caseworkers.

In addition, several teen-age girls from the neighborhood are working in the project as aides in the nursery areas. It is interesting to note that their participation in this program and interaction with the staff has led to an improvement in their own personal appearance as well as an increased level of interest in learning.

A broad range of measurements, including efforts to assess the socioeconomic levels of the families, has been incorporated in the Chicago experimental design. Control, or comparison, groups have been established so that relative progress can be determined. The feasibility of integrating an educational program into a public welfare agency has been successfully demonstrated and should facilitate the replication of such a project by a welfare agency in another community.

The Greeley Project

The Greeley, Colorado, demonstration project, directed by Dr. Glen Nimnicht assisted by Dr. John Meier, includes forty-five environmentally deprived Spanish-American three- and four-year-old children in the experimental groups. The project is almost completely nonautomated. It utilizes the same general responsive environment process as the other two projects, but differs significantly in that it does not have computerized "talking typewriters." The Greeley project uses an electric typewriter, and a responsive attendant simulates the "talking typewriter." The attendants are specially trained to respond to the children's activities as they discover the relationship between visual, auditory, and kinesthetic (use of three-dimensional letters) symbols.

A major accomplishment of the project has been the generation of a number of responsive environment methods and techniques related to personality development of culturally and environmentally deprived children. Pedagogical methods of Montessori, Piaget, Moore, Deutsch, and others are employed insofar as they meet the operational criteria of an autotelic responsive environment. It is exciting to see children of Mexican-American descent from woefully inadequate home environments describing to an attendant, over the telephone and in understandable English, the dress-up costumes they are wearing; or to see a group of children participating in a game in which they correctly select words printed on cards and then insert the cards into a simple machine (Language Master) that says the words aloud.

The Greeley project has been preparing video-taped teaching episodes that are also put on 16-mm color film so that they can be widely disseminated through OEO to Head Start and other training programs, such as the Head Start Follow-Through program. These teaching episodes will enable teachers to hear and see the responsive environment project at work, and not only observe the methodology for themselves but facilitate their own application of some of the concepts and procedures.

The experimental design of the Greeley project has provided for the measurement of a great many variables for both experimental and comparison groups. In addition, some new measurement instruments and techniques have been designed that will enable educators of very young children to measure the effects of their methods and techniques.

This project is being further extended to NDEA teacher programs, and is being applied extensively to early-learning problems of Indian children on reservations.

GENERAL CONSIDERATIONS

The efforts in actually applying the responsive environment process to children in everyday educational settings are just beginning. Only very small numbers of children have been exposed to the responsive environment concept of education. There are many questions to be answered, and indeed, probably many questions yet to be asked. Extensive research and evaluation, hopefully resulting in modifications and improvements of techniques, needs to be undertaken. Of the many questions that remain, some of the most significant are:

(1) What social work techniques are most supportive to this new educational system?

(2) What effect does the responsive environment concept have on the overall curriculum in the participating schools?

(3) What effect will this system have on the administration of the school? How can schools be helped to adjust to the new system?

(4) What effect might the process have on traditional tests and measurements and on conventional grading systems?

(5) What are the plant requirements of the system?

(6) How can we make maximum utilization of both the automated and the nonautomated equipment?

(7) What is the feasibility of an intermediate step between the talking typewriter and the traditional classroom, such as computer-assisted instruction, or a multimedia systems approach to early education?

(8) What is the most cost-effective utilization of the responsive environment concepts and approaches? Can it be economical for a school system?

(9) How can a school system best make a transition to a responsive environment system?

These questions cannot be answered easily or quickly. An effort must be made to determine how the advantages accruing from these projects can be made available to the greatest number of pupils. Careful cost analyses must be made of the automated and the nonautomated equipment, including teacher-pupil ratios and teacher-training costs. Preliminary indications are that the much less expensive, nonautomated equipment in the hands of well-trained teacher aides (booth attendants) can be as effective as the automated equipment. On the other hand, the training of sufficient teachers and teacher aides can itself become a formidable and possibly insurmountable program. Programs for teacher and attendant training and retraining on a massive scale must be made. Probably both approaches—automated and nonautomated—will be required in varying degrees in different settings.

However, even in the face of many unanswered questions, there seems to be no doubt that the concept of a responsive environment approach to early education can contribute significantly to the education of all children.

Dr. Gabriel Ofiesh
Dr. Ruth Ann O'Keefe

The authors acknowledge the assistance of A. J. Bouck, Dr. P. Ransohoff and M. Durland, all members of the staff of the Early Learning Laboratory Center for Educational Technology, The Catholic University of America, Washington, D.C.

REFERENCES

[1] LeRoy Aserlind, "A Conjectural Approach to Design and Development of Special Education Instructional Materials." *Education and Training of the Mentally Retarded*, 2:59–62 (April, 1967).

[2] *Business Automation* (Automation Education Edition), pp. 46AE–49AE, April, 1967.

[3] Omar K. Moore, "Autotelic Responsive Environments and Exceptional Children," in J. Hellmuth, ed., *The Special Child* in *Century 21*. (Seattle, Special Child Publications, 1964).

SUGGESTED READINGS

Bushnell, Don, and Allen, Dwight, eds., *The Computer in American Education*. New York, Wiley, 1967.

Deutsch, M., "The Disadvantaged Child and the Learning Process," in A.H. Passow, ed., *Education in Depressed Areas*. New York, Teacher's College, Columbia, 1963, pp. 163–179.

Deutsch, M., "Minority Group and Class Status as Related to Social and Personality Factors in Scholastic Achievement." *Monograph, Society for Applied Anthropology*, 1960, No. 2.

Eraut, M., "An Instructional Systems Approach to Course Development." *AV Communication Review*, 15:92–101 (Spring, 1967).

Gentile, J. Ronald, "The First Generation of Computer-Assisted Instructional Systems: An Evaluative Review." *AV Communication Review*, 15:23–53 (Spring, 1967).

Goodlad, John, O'Toole, John Jr., and Tyler, Louise, *Computers and Informations Systems in Education*. New York, Harcourt, Brace & World, 1966.

Gordon, E.W., "Characteristics of Socially Disadvantaged Children." *Rev. Educ. Res.*, Vol. 35 (1965), pp. 377–388.

Gotkin, L.G., *et al.*, "Standard Telephone Interview." Unpublished memo report. New York, Institute for Developmental Studies, 1964.

Meier, J.H., "An Exploratory Factor Analysis of Psychodiagnostic and Case Study Information from Children in Special Education Classes for the Educable Mentally Handicapped." Unpublished dissertation. Ann Arbor, Mich., University Microfilms, 1965.

————, "Rationale for the Use of Micro-training with Teachers, Counselors and Learners." Greeley, Colo., Rocky Mountain Educational Laboratory, 1966b.

————, "The Use of Videotape Recording Media for Learning: Problem-solving Strategies and Ameliorating Self-concept." Greeley, Colo., Psycho-Educational Research Institute. Unpublished paper, 1966c.

Nimnicht, G.P., and Meier, J.H., "First Year Partial Progress Report of a Project in Autotelic Responsive Environment Nursery School for Environmentally Deprived Spanish-surnamed Children." Greeley, Colo., Colorado State College Bureau of Educational Research, *The Journal of Research Services*, Vol. 5, No. 2, Fall, 1966, 305-item bibliography.

Ofiesh, Gabriel, and Meierhenry, Wesley, eds., *Trends in Programmed Instruction*, Department of Audio-visual Instruction, NEA, 1201 16th St., N.W., Washington, D.C. 20036 (1964).

Piaget, J., *The Growth of Logical Thinking in the Child*. New York, Basic Books, 1958.

Riessman, F., *The Culturally Deprived Child*. New York, Harper & Row, 1962.

Schrag, Peter, "Kids, Computers, and Corporations." *Saturday Review*, May 20, 1967.

Silberman, Charles, "Technology Is Knocking at the Schoolhouse Door." *Fortune*, August, 1966.

OTHER SOURCES OF INFORMATION

Association for Educational Data Systems (AEDS), 1201 16 Street NW, Washington, D.C. 20036.

Association for Computing Machinery, 211 East 43rd Street, New York, N.Y. 10017.

National Society for Programmed Instruction, Trinity University, 715 Stadium Drive, San Antonio, Texas 78212.

Educational Technology, 35 Church Street, Patterson, N.J.

Department of Audio Visual Instruction (DAVI), NEA, 1201 16th Street, NW, Washington, D.C. 20036.

*Science Research Associates publishes several series of booklets
containing new ideas and methods in education, for in-service training
of teachers. One such booklet is* The Montessori Approach to
Education *by June Heinrich, who writes: "One of the great advantages
of the Montessori approach is that it gives every child (whether
categorized as retarded, average, or gifted) the chance to learn at his
own pace within a class of children of all abilities."**

*She believes that Montessori classes for culturally disadvantaged
children are likely to become very numerous in the future as we attempt
to realize the American dream of a good education for every child
regardless of his background.*

EXPLORING AND EXPANDING MONTESSORI:
A GUIDE TO ACTION

The evaluations of Montessori by Dr. Banta, Dr. Argy, and other
researchers discussed in this book, and the practical implementation
of Montessori by Mrs. Gitter, Mrs. Rietz, and others, also reported
herein, indicate that Montessori methodology has much to offer
normal, handicapped, and deprived children. Indeed, as already
noted, Montessori herself worked successfully with all three types of
children.

Therefore, those who work directly with children, or are responsible at any level for programs affecting children, would do well to
investigate Montessori possibilities.

Parents, public education personnel, college and university
educators, graduate students, researchers, and program planners
can take such courses of action as the following:

---

* June Heinrich, *The Montessori Approach to Education.* Unit Three, Series I.
SRA Teacher Education Extension Service. Chicago, Science Research Associates, 1967, p. 13.

PARENTS

Read books by and about Montessori and her work.

Join the local Montessori study group; organize one if none is available.

Support Montessori associations, such as the American Montessori Society and the Association Montessori Internationale.

Enroll children in a Montessori school; organize one if none is available.

Practice Montessori principles in the home. (See *Montessori for the Disadvantaged* for practical tips for *all* parents of young children.)

Work to see that some Montessori classes are instituted in the local public school system, such as Montessori kindergarten or classes for special children.

PUBLIC SCHOOL TEACHERS

Pursue the Montessori philosophy in the classroom.

Make or purchase some of the less complex Montessori materials for use in the classroom.

Initiate some Montessori activities in the classroom, such as the "exercises of practical life."

Establish a dialogue with local Montessori teachers.

Take some Montessori training. Opportunities range from short seminars to training programs of several years.

PUBLIC SCHOOL BOARDS OF EDUCATION, ADMINISTRATORS, AND SUPERVISORS

Set up Montessori in-service training (workshops, seminars, courses, etc.) for teachers and other staff.

Organize pilot Montessori classes in the schools. Hire trained Montessori teachers.

Utilize Montessori consultants.

COLLEGE AND UNIVERSITY TEACHER TRAINERS; STATE DEPARTMENT OF EDUCATION STAFF*

Establish a Montessori method introductory survey course, for credit.

Develop a sequence of courses in Montessori theory and practice leading to a major or degree in Montessori.

Organize demonstration Montessori classes for observation by education students.

Have students visit local Montessori schools.

Place books by and about Montessori on required reading lists as basic or supplementary texts.

Organize Montessori study centers stocked with books, tapes, films, etc.

Invite Montessori experts to speak to classes of education students.

GRADUATE STUDENTS, RESEARCHERS, PROGRAM PLANNERS

Submit research proposals with Montessori components to foundations, government agencies, and other funding sources.

Prepare reports, theses, and dissertations on Montessori subjects.

Build Montessori components into nursery, day-care, "War on Poverty" and other educational and social action programs.

---

* An encouraging development is the increasing trend toward accreditation of Montessori teacher training by state departments of education. For example, the Midwest Montessori Teacher Training Center of Chicago, organized by Dr. Urban Fleege, Professor of Child Development at DePaul University, is now approved by the Illinois Department of Public Instruction. It also meets the requirements of the U.S. Veterans Administration, which means that qualified veterans can now receive government financial assistance for Montessori training leading to an American Montessori Society Diploma.

REVIEW

The Montessori method, in a nutshell, involves (1) the *child as an independent learner* interacting with (2) the *prepared environment* featuring (3) the *"new teacher" as observer*. The goal of (4) the *learning process* as *autoeducation* is the emergence of (5) a *"new man"* able to cope with today's complex world. These five key facets of the Montessori approach are briefly reviewed below:

1. CHILD AS INDEPENDENT LEARNER

Motivated to develop himself, utilizing his formative period, absorbent mind, and sensitive periods.

As explorer, displays remarkable powers of concentration in making discoveries in his world leading to mastery of himself and environment.

2. PREPARED ENVIRONMENT

Organized to provide child with interesting materials and milieu of liberty for autoeducation.

Designed to promote expansion of child's physical, emotional, intellectual, and social life.

3. NEW TEACHER

Teacher as trained observer who teaches indirectly, intervening only when necessary.

Teacher as scientist prepared in spirit as well as mechanical skill to conduct learning experiments in her classroom laboratory.

4. LEARNING PROCESS AS AUTOEDUCATION

Sensory, motor, and language education with programmed materials encouraging individual self-choice and self-pacing.

Multisensory, intrinsically motivated sequential activity with flexible scheduling and grouping, and cosmic curriculum.

5. "NEW MAN"

Independent yet socially aware individual who is self-disciplined, confident, competent, spontaneous, creative, and psychologically fully functioning.

Inner harmony growing from release of, respect for, and response to human potential for perceptual proficiency, motor coordination and intellectual development leading to internal order of "prepared mind."

Lloyd Dunn, editor of *Exceptional Children in the Schools*, lists seven categories of such children, which include those with:

1. intellectual limitations
2. superior intellect
3. behavior problems
4. speech problems
5. impaired hearing
6. impaired vision
7. neurological and nonsensory impairments

These categories can be subdivided into various types. Within category one, for example, we can identify (a) the slow learner, (b) the educable mentally retarded, (c) the trainable mentally retarded. But whatever the type of exceptionality, such components of the Montessori approach as the following, in varying combinations and adapted as necessary to the unique needs of the individual child, are proving effective:

1. *Sensory education* and *training in observation*, leading toward the objectives of *perceptual preciseness* and *cognitive clarity*.

2. *Preparation* for and *practice* with *sequential sensorimotor-intellectual materials* and *activities* to *develop proficiency* in the sensory, motor, and intellectual areas.

3. *Individualized "autoeducation"* featuring *self-paced progress indirectly assists child* in process of forming his unique self.

4. *Completing cycles of activity and work* involving *freedom of movement*, and *manual activity* with *manipulatable Montessori materials*.

5. A *balance of liberty with limits* and *spontaneity with order*, as the child's *conquest of freedom* leads to *independence* and *self-discipline*.

6. *Prepared environment* to match the child's developmental needs during his *sensitive periods* with interesting materials containing *control of error* enabling him to teach himself.

7. *New teacher* as *exemplary observer* and *communicator*, conducting *pedagogical experiments* in the *learning laboratory* of the prepared environment.

Appendices

APPENDIX A
MONTESSORI LECTURES ON SPECIAL EDUCATION

The following material is an edited summary of selected lectures on pedagogy delivered by Montessori to teachers of Rome attending a course at the State Orthophrenic School in 1900. A number of other physicians were lecturing on such subjects as psychology, while Montessori had reserved for herself the development and teaching of a special pedagogy for defective children "along the lines previously laid down by Itard and Seguin."

Outline:

> General Rules
> Muscular Education
> Education of the Senses
> Simultaneous Reading and Writing of Words
> Grammar
> Object Lessons
> History
> Geography
> Mathematics

GENERAL RULES

To attract the attention of defective children, strong sensory stimulants are necessary. The lessons, therefore, should be eminently practical. Every lesson should begin with the presentation of the object to be illustrated by the teacher in a few words distinctly pronounced with continual modulations of the voice and accompanied by vivid imitative expression. The lessons should be made as attractive as possible and, as far as practicable, presented as games, to arouse the curiosity of the child: guessing games, blindman's buff, storekeeping, etc. But however amusing the game may be, the lesson should always be stopped while the child is still willing to continue. His attention, which is easily fatigued, should never be exhausted. To fix ideas, lessons should be repeated many times. Each time, however, the same objects should be presented under different forms and in a different environment, so that it will always be interesting by appearing as something new: storytelling, living tableaux, large illustrations, colored pictures, audiovisual aids, etc. In case individual teaching is necessary, as happens in the most elementary classes, care should be exercised to keep all the other children busy with different toys: insets, lacing-and-buttoning frames, hooks and eyes, etc. When children refuse to take part in their lessons it is better not to use coercion, but to aim at obtaining obedience indirectly through the child's imitation of his schoolmates. Glowing praise of the pupils who are showing good will in their work almost always brings the recalcitrants to time. When a child shows he has understood the point under discussion, it is better not to ask for a repetition. His attention is easily fatigued, and the second time he may say badly what at first he gave successfully; and the failure may discourage him. It is well to be satisfied with the first good answer, bestow such praise as will afford the child a pleasant memory of what he has been doing, and go back to the subject on the following day, or, at the earliest, several hours later.

In manual training, however, the situation is different. The lesson in this subject can be a whole hour long and should take the form of serious work and not of play. The child should be set early at some useful task, even if a little hard work, not unattended with risk, be involved (wood-working, etc.). From the outset, thus, the child will become familiar with the challenges of bread-winning effort and will learn to meet them.

Interest in work may be stimulated by appropriate rewards. The child may earn during work hours the money for his purchases at the store, for his tickets to the play and the film. The child who does not work may be kept away from the more attractive lessons, such as dancing and music, which come immediately after the work hour. As a matter of fact, these children take to manual training very readily, provided the tasks assigned are adapted to the natural inclinations of the individual child in such a way that he may take the greatest possible satisfaction in his work and thus by natural bent attain a skill useful to himself and society.

MUSCULAR EDUCATION

Muscular education has for its object the bringing of the individual to some labor useful for society. This labor must always be executed by means of the muscles, whether it be manual labor, speaking, or writing. In a word, the intelligence must bring the muscles under control and therefore the muscles must be prepared by an education that will reduce them to coordination. Muscular education in defectives accordingly has for its object the stimulation and co-ordination of useful movements.

(1) The child is taught to become acquainted with himself. The various parts of his body are pointed out to him and he is asked to touch them. This continues up to the point of distinguishing right from left. Begin with the larger members of the body (arms, legs, trunk, head) to be named in connection with movements of the whole body. Then pass to the smaller members (the fingers, knuckles, the organs of the mouth), to be referred to respectively in the education of the hand and in the teaching of speech.

(2) The child is taught coordinated movements relating to gymnastics (walking, running, jumping, pushing, etc.).

(3) Movements relating: (a) to the simpler form of manual labor (exercises of practical life: washing, dressing, picking up and laying down various objects, opening and closing drawers); (b) to more complex kinds of manual labor (elements of various trades, weaving, Froebel exercises, etc.).

(4) Movements relating to articulate language. For this educational process the following general rules are to be followed: first, movements of the whole body must precede movements of specific parts; second, only by analyzing complex movements in their successive stages and by working out their details point by point can we arrive at the execution of a perfect complex movement. For example, in the combination drawing-writing exercise, the child is

given a sheet on which appear a circle and a square in outline. The circle is filled in with a red pencil, the square with blue (insets). Smaller and smaller circles are next given, also circles and triangles. They are variously disposed on the page. They are to be filled in with colored pencils. Then comes the tracing. The black lines are followed around with colored pencils: the circle, the triangle, the square. This comes easily to the child who has been taught to trace with the wooden pointer the figures outlined on the inset charts. Writing follows immediately on the exercises in tracing with the pointer on the charts of the written alphabet. Some help can be given the child by having him darken with a black pencil the letter written on the copybook by the teacher. As the child writes, his attention should be directed to the fact that he is writing on a limited plane surface; that he begins at the top, moving from left to right and little by little coming down the page.

As soon as the child has learned to identify the letters and also to write them, he is asked to pronounce them. Then the alphabet is arranged in phonetic order. This order is to be varied according to individual defects made apparent while the child is pronouncing spontaneously the sounds of the consonants or vowels, or the words illustrating the consonants on the charts. We begin by showing the child and having him pronounce, first, syllables and, then, words that contain the letters he is able to pronounce well. Then we go on to the sounds he has trouble with, finally to those he cannot pronounce at all (linguistic correction). In primary schools, speech correction should be in the hands of a specially trained teacher, like gymnastics, manual training, and singing.

EDUCATION OF THE SENSES

Outline for examination.

Sight: Sense of color. It is necessary to call the attention of the child several times to the same color by presenting it to him under different aspects and in different environments. The stimulus should be strong. Whenever the teacher gives an idea she should unite with it the word, the only word that is related to the idea. The words should be emphatically and distinctly pronounced.

(1) Pedagogical aprons: The colors are presented on a large moving surface, as, for instance, an apron worn by the teacher— *e.g.*, a red apron. The teacher points to it, touches it, lifting it with noticeable movements of the arms, continually calls the attention of the child to it. "Look! See here! Attention!" and so on; then saying in a low voice and slowly, "This is [and then in a louder voice] red, red, red! ! !" Now take two aprons, one red, the other blue; repeat the same process for the blue. There are three stages in the process of distinguishing between colors: (a) "This is . . . red!" (b) "Your apron is red!" (c) "What color is this?" Then try three aprons, red, blue, and yellow, bordered with white and black.

(2) Insets—color and form. The red circle, the blue square. There are three stages: (a) "This is red, red, red! Touch it! Do you feel? Your finger goes all the way around, all the way around. It is round, it is round, all round. Put it in its place!" (b) "Give me the red one!" (c) "What color is this circle?"

(3) The dark room. A Bengal red color is shown: "It is red!" The color appears behind a circular disc: "It is red!" The blue is shown behind a square window: "It is blue, blue, blue," etc.

(4) The child is given a circular tablet of red sugar to eat and a square lump of blue sugar. He is made to smell a red piece of cloth strongly scented with musk; or a blue piece of cloth scented with asafetida, etc.

(5) The color chart.

(6) The first game of Froebel.

The first pedagogical material given should contain the color already taught. The notion of color should be associated with its original environment.

Shapes: Solids, insets. The procedure is always in the three stages mentioned. (1) Show the object to the child. (2) Have him recognize it. (3) Have him give it its name.

Dimensions: Rods of the same thickness, but of graduated length. First the longest and shortest are shown. The child is asked to touch them and interchange them: "Pick up the longest!" "Place it on the table!" etc. Repeat this exercise, adding some intermediate lengths; again, finally, with all the rods. Next the rods may be disarranged; the child is to put them back in order of length. Notice whether the child makes an accurate choice in the confused pile of the graduated dimensions; or whether it is only by placing two rods together that he comes to notice the difference between them. Notice how long it is before the child makes an accurate choice in the pile and of what degrees of difference in length he is accurately aware.

Try the same exercise for thickness: prisms of equal length, but of graduated thickness, using the same procedure in analogous exercises. Games may be used for the estimation of distances.

The tactile sense proper: One board with a corrugated surface (like a grater) and one smooth. Another board with five adjacent surfaces of graduated roughness. Similar exercises may be used in the feeling of cloths (guessing games).

Games: The child is blindfolded and lightly tickled. He must seize what is tickling him, putting his hand rapidly to the irritant. ("Fly catching," a game for the localization of stimulants.)

$$\text{liquids} \begin{cases} \text{astringents} \\ \text{glues} \\ \text{oils} \end{cases}$$

Tactile muscular sense:

$$\left. \begin{array}{l} \text{elastic bodies} \\ \\ \text{nonresilient bodies} \end{array} \right\} \text{balls} \begin{cases} \text{rubber} \\ \\ \text{wooden} \end{cases}$$

Use skins, leather gloves, and various kinds of cloths for feeling.

The muscular sense: Balls of the same appearance, but of graduated weights. Differentiation of coins by weight.

The stereognostic sense: Recognition of elementary forms, of rare objects, of coins.

Thermal senses: Hot liquids, iced liquids; relative warmth of linen and wool, wood, wax, metal.

Olfactory sense: Asafetida, oil of rose, mint, etc.

$$\text{odors of} \begin{cases} \text{tobacco smoke} \\ \text{burned sugar} \\ \text{incense} \\ \text{burned maple} \end{cases}$$

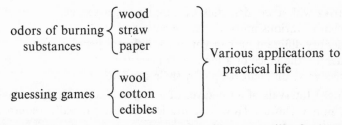

odors of burning substances { wood / straw / paper }

guessing games { wool / cotton / edibles }

Various applications to practical life

Odors of foods (practical life): fresh milk, sour milk; fresh meat, stale meat; rancid butter, fresh butter, etc.

Taste: The four fundamental tastes (guessing games). Instructive applications to practice in the kitchen and at meals.

Tastes of various food substances:

exercises of practical life { milk gruel (milk and flour) / diluted wine / sweet wine / turned wine (vinegar), etc. }

The practice of the senses begins in the lower classes in the form of guessing games; in the higher classes the education of the senses is applied to exercises of practical life.

Hearing: Empirical measurement of the acuteness of the sense of hearing. Specimen game: the teacher about 35 feet away from the blindfolded children, and standing where an object has been hidden, whispers the words "Find it!" Those who have heard her will be able to find the object. Having removed from the line the children who have heard, the teacher steps to another place about a yard nearer and repeats the experiment to the children who are left over, etc.

Intensity of sound:

Throw to the floor metal blocks of various sizes, coins of graduated weight.

Strike glasses one after the other according to size.

Ring bells of graduated size.

Quality of sound: Produce different sounds and noises.

     Bells of metal
     Bells of terracotta
     Open bells
     Closed bells

Strike with a wooden stick on tin plates, glasses, etc.

Identify various musical instruments.

Identify different human voices (of different people).

Identify the voice of a man, a woman, a child.

Recognize different people by their step, etc.

Pitch: Intervals of an octave, of a major triad, and so on; major and minor chords. However, musical education really requires a separate chapter.

Sound projection, localization of sound in space: The child is blindfolded. The sound is produced: (1) in front of him; behind him; to the right; to the left; above his head; (2) the blindfolded child recognizes the relative distance at which the sounds are produced; (3) the child decides from which side of the room the sounds come; he is made to follow someone who is speaking.

The horizontal plane: This is the first notion imparted to the child concerning his relationship to the objects about him. Almost all the objects the child may perceive around him with his senses rest on the horizontal plane: his table, his chair, and so on. The very objects on which the child sits or puts his toys are horizontal planes. If the plane were not horizontal, the object would fall, but they would strike on the floor which, again, is a horizontal plane. Place an object on the child's table and tip one end of the table to show him that the object falls.

Guessing game for the plane surface: This game serves to fix the notion of the plane surface and at the same time trains the eye and the attention of the child.

1. Under one of three aluminum cups is placed a small red ball, a cherry, or a piece of candy. The child must remember under which cup the object is hidden. The teacher tries herself and fails, always raising the empty cups and returning them to their places. The child, however, finds the object immediately.

2. The teacher now begins to move the three cups about on the plane surface. The child has to keep his eye on his cup and never lose sight of it.

3. Repeat this exercise with six cups.

Checkerboard game: This serves to teach the child the limits and the various divisions of a plane. The squares are large and in black and white. The whole board should be surrounded by a border in relief. Various points are indicated on the plane: forward, backward, right, left, center, by placing a tin soldier at each point indicated. The soldiers may be moved about by the child in obedience to directions of the teacher: "The officer on horseback to the center"; "Standard-bearer to the right," etc.! Finally, make all the soldiers advance toward the center of the board over the black squares only; then over the white squares only, etc.

These notions may be applied to exercises of practical life. The children already know how to set the table without thinking of what they are doing. From now on, the teacher may say: "Put the plates on the plane surface of the tables." "Put the bottle to the left! In the center!" etc. Have a small table set with little dishes, having the objects arranged in obedience to commands of the teacher. After this, we may proceed to the Froebel games on the plane surface with the cubes, blocks, and so on.

Inset game as a preparation for reading, drawing, and writing: After the child knows the different colors and shapes in the inset, the color tablets of the big inset can be put in place: (1) on a piece of cardboard where the figures have been drawn in shading in the respective colors; (2) on a cardboard where the same figures have been drawn merely in colored outline (linear abstraction of a regular figure).

Inset of shapes where the pieces are all of the same color (blue): The child recognizes the shape and puts the pieces in place: (1) on a cardboard where the figure is shaded; (2) on a cardboard where the figure is merely outlined (linear abstraction of regular geometrical figures). Meanwhile, the child has been touching the pieces: "The tablet is smooth. It turns round and round and round. It is a circle. Here we have a square. You go this way and there is a point; this way, and there is another point, and another, and another; there are four points! In the triangle there are three points!" Then the child follows with his finger the figures outlined on the cardboard. "This one is entirely round: it is a circle! This one has four points: it is a square! This one has three points: it is a triangle!" The child runs over the same figures with a small rod of wood (pointer), etc.

SIMULTANEOUS READING AND WRITING OF WORDS

The child, through sensory education, has acquired some notions of color, shape, surface (smooth and rough), smell, taste, etc. At the same time, he has learned to count (one, two, three, four points). Uniting all possible notions concerning a single object, we arrive at his first concrete idea of the object itself: the object lesson. To the idea thus acquired, we give the word that represents the object. Just as the concrete idea results from the assembling of acquired notions, so the word results from the union of known sounds, the perceived symbols.

At this point, we may bring in the chart with the vowels, painted red. The child sees "irregular figures outlined in color." Give the child the vowels made of red wood. He is to place them on the corresponding figures of the chart. He is made to touch the wooden vowels, running his finger around them in the way they are written. They are called by their names. The vowels are arranged according to similarity in shape (reading):

o e a

i u

Then the child is commanded: "Show me the letter O! Put it in its place!" Then he is asked: "What letter is this?" It will be found at this point that many children make a mistake, if they merely look at the letter, but guess rightly when they touch it. It is possible accordingly to distinguish the various individual types, visual, motoric, etc.

Next, the child is made to touch the letter outlined on the chart, first with his forefinger only, then with the fore and middle fingers, finally with a little wooden pointer to be held like a pen. The letter must always be followed around in the way it is written.

The consonants are drawn in blue and arranged on various charts, according to similarity in shape (reading, writing). The moveable alphabet in blue wood is added to this. The letters are to be superimposed on the chart as was done for the vowels. Along with the alphabet we have another series of charts, where, beside the consonant identical with the wooden letter, there are painted one or more figures of objects, the names of which begin with the letter in question. Beside the longhand letter, there is also painted in the same color a smaller letter in print type. The teacher, naming the consonants in the phonic method, points to the letter, then to the chart, pronouncing the name of the objects that are painted there, and stressing the first letter: *e.g.*, "M ... Man ... M: Give me M!" "Put it where it belongs!" "Follow around it with your finger!" Here the linguistic defects of the children may be studied.

The child, in looking at the letters, identifying them, and tracing them in the way they are written, is preparing himself both for reading and writing at the same time. The two processes are exactly extemporaneous. Touching them and looking at them brings several senses to bear on the fixing of the image. Later the two acts are separated: first, looking (reading), then touching (writing). According to their respective type, some children learn to read first, others to write first.

Reading lesson: On the teacher's table is the large stand for the movable alphabet in black printed letters. The teacher arranges on it the vowels and a few consonants. Each child, in his own place, has the small movable alphabet in a pasteboard box. The children take from the box the same letters they see on the large stand, and arrange them in the same order. The teacher takes up some object that has a simple word for a name, *e.g.*, "bread." She calls the attention of the child to the object, reviewing an objective lesson already learned, thus arousing the child's interest in the object. "Shall we write the word 'bread'?" "Hear how I say it!" "See how I say it!" The teacher pronounces separately and distinctly the sounds of the letters that make up the word, exaggerating the movements of the vocal organs so that they are plainly visible to the children. As the pupils repeat the word they continue their education in speaking.

A child now comes to the teacher's desk to choose the letters corresponding to the sounds and tries to arrange them in the order in which they appear in the word. The children do the same with the small letters at their seats. Every mistake gives rise to a correction useful to the whole class. The teacher repeats the word in front of each one who has made a mistake, trying to get the child to correct himself. When all the children have arranged their letters properly, the teacher shows a card (visiting-card size) on which is printed (in print-type letters about a centimeter high) the word "bread." All the children are made to read it. Then some child is asked to put the card where he finds the word written before him; next, on the object the word stands for. The process is repeated with two or three other objects, with their respective names: "bread," "lamp," "peas." Then the teacher gathers up the cards from the various objects, shuffles them, and calls on some child: "Which object do you like best?" "Bread!" "Find me the card with the word 'bread.'" When the card has been selected, all the children are asked to read it: "Is Mary right in saying that this is the word 'bread'?" "Put the card back where it belongs!" (*i.e.*, on its object). In the subsequent lessons, the old cards, with the objects they stand for removed, should be mixed with the new ones. From the entire pack the children are to select the new cards and place them on their objects. A primary reading book ought to present these words next to a picture of the object for which they stand.

In this way the children are taught to associate objects with words. When they have been taught to make the syllable, the reading lesson may be continued without the use of objects, though it is still preferable to use words that will, if possible, have a concrete meaning for the children.

Writing: The children are already able to use the cursive (writing) alphabet, which corresponds to the small letter (print-type) that is neither "touched" nor written, but is merely read. They must now write in handwriting, and place close together, the little letters that they have assembled in the movable alphabet to compose words. As each word is read or written for every object lesson, for every action, printed cards are being assembled that will later be used to make clauses and sentences with movable words that may be moved about just as the individual letters were moved about in making the words themselves. Later on, the simple clauses or sentences should refer to actions performed by the children. The first step should be to bring two or more words together: *e.g.*, red wool, sweet candy, four-footed dog, etc. Then we may go on to the sentence itself: The wool is red; The soup is hot; The dog has four feet; Mary eats the candy, etc. The children first compose the sentences with their cards; then they copy them in their writing books. To facilitate the choice of the cards, they are arranged in special boxes; for instance, one box is labeled "noun"; or its compartments are distinguished thus: "food," "clothing," "animals," "people," etc. There should be a box for adjectives with compartments for "colors," "shapes," "qualities," etc. There should be another for "particles," "conjunctions," "prepositions," etc. A box should be reserved for actions with the label "verbs" above; and then in it a compartment should be reserved for the "infinitive," "present," "past," and "future" respectively. The children gradually learn by practice to take their cards from the boxes and put them back in their proper places. They soon learn to know their "word boxes" and they readily find the cards they want among the colors, shapes, qualities, etc., or among animals, foods, etc. Ultimately the teacher will find occasion to explain the meaning of the big words at the top of the drawers— "noun," "adjective," "verb," etc., and this will be the first step into the subject of grammar.

GRAMMAR

Noun Lesson

We may call persons and objects by their name (their noun). People answer if we call them; so do animals. Inanimate objects, however, never answer, because they cannot; but if they could answer, they would; for example, if I say "Mary," Mary answers; if I say "peas," the peas do not answer, because they cannot. You children do understand when I call an object and you bring it to me. I say, for example, "book, beans, peas." If I don't tell you the name of the object, you don't understand what I am talking about because every object has a different name. This name is the word that stands for the object. This name is a noun. When I mention a noun you understand immediately the object that the noun represents: tree, chair, pen, book, lamb, etc. If I do not give this noun, you do not know what I am talking about; for, if I say simply, "Bring me . . . at once, I want it," you do not know what I want unless I tell you the name of the object. Unless I give you the noun, tell you the name of the object. Unless I give you the noun, you do not understand. Thus every object is represented by a word that is its name and this name is a noun. To understand whether a word is a noun or not, you simply ask, "Is it a thing?" "Would it answer if I spoke to it?" "Could I carry it to the teacher?" For instance, bread. Yes, bread is an object; table, yes, it is an object; conductor, yes, the conductor would answer, if I were to speak to him.

Let us look through our cards now. I take several cards from different boxes and shuffle them. Here is the word "sweet." Bring me "sweet." Is there anything to answer when I call "sweet?" But you are bringing me a piece of candy! I didn't say "candy": I said "sweet"! And now you have given me sugar! I said "sweet." If I say "candy" or "sugar," then you understand what I want, what object I am thinking about, because the words "candy" and "sugar" stand for objects. Those words are nouns. Now let us look through the noun cards. Let us read a couple of lines in our reading books and see whether there are any nouns there. Tell me, are there any nouns? How are we to find some nouns? Look around you! Look at yourself, your clothes! Name every object that you see! Every word you thus pronounce will be a noun: teacher, clothing, necktie, chair, class, children, books, etc. Just look at this picture that represents so many things! The figures represent persons and objects. Name each of these figures! Every word you pronounce will be a noun!

Verb: Action

Mary, rise from your seat! Walk! Mary has performed a number of actions. She has risen. She has performed the action of rising. She has walked. Walk stands for an action. Now write your name on the blackboard! Writing is an action. Erase what you have written. Erasing is an action. When I spoke to Mary, I performed the action of speaking. (Just as the noun was taught with objects, here we must have actions.)

The next step will be to suggest a little exercise of imagination. Look at all these objects! Try to imagine some action that each might perform! A class, for instance; what actions might a class perform? Store: what actions might take place in a store? Let us now look through our cards after we have shuffled them. Next try our reading book. Show me which of the words are verbs. Give me some words that are verbs (infinitives).

Present, past, future. I am performing an action now. Have I performed it before? Did I do it yesterday? Have I always done it in the past? When I walk now, I say I am walking, I walk. When I mean the action that I performed yesterday, I say: I was walking, I walked. The same action performed at different times is described differently. How interesting that is! The word referring to an object never changes. The beads are beads today. They were beads yesterday. Actions, however, are represented by words that change according to the time in which they are performed. Today I walk. Yesterday I walked. Tomorrow I shall walk. It is always I who do the walking, I who perform the action of walking; and I walk always in the same way, putting one foot in front of the other. The objects you see perform an action always perform it. Do you see that little bird that is flying—that is performing the action of flying? It was flying yesterday. It flew at some time in the past. Tomorrow also, that is, at some future time, if the little bird lives, it will fly and it will fly always in the same way, beating its wings to and fro. You see what an interesting thing a verb is! It changes its words according to the time in which the action is performed. It is different according as it represents action in present time, or action in past time, or action in future time. Now, see! I am going to take out some of my cards and make up a little sentence:

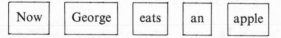

Now I am going to change the word that stands for the time when the action takes place. In place of the card "now" I am going to use this one:

Is this a good sentence? No! Supposing we change the time of the verb: Yesterday George ate an apple. This makes good sense. Put these cards back now in the boxes where they belong.

Adjective

Every object possesses certain qualities. Tell me what you can about this apple. It is red, it is round, it is sweet. What qualities can you find in this chair? It is hard, it is brown, it is wooden. What about your schoolmates, the children? Are they good, are they pretty, are they polite, are they obedient, or are they naughty, impolite, disobedient, disorderly? Let us look through our cards to see whether we can find words that stand for the qualities of objects. Supposing we select some from the drawer of the adjective and some from the drawer of the noun. Now let us place beside each noun a card that makes sense with it: here, for instance, I have Charles, red, quadruped, transparent. Does that mean anything? Well, then, find me some adjectives that will go well with Charles. Adjectives are words that stand for qualities of a given object. They must go well with their noun. Find me some adjectives that fit well with the noun "dog." They must be words that stand for some quality of the dog. Now put all the cards back in the compartments where they belong. (This latter exercise is very instructive.)

In this method of teaching grammar we make use of objects and actions directly relating to life. Such lessons may be made more attractive with storytelling, etc. The teaching of grammar at this period should be extended as far as is possible without forcing the pupil.

OBJECT LESSONS

There should be concise and vivid descriptions of some object. The attention of the child should be sustained by changing the tone of voice, by exclamations calculated to excite the child's curiosity, by praise, etc. Never begin with the word, but always with the object. All the notions possessed by the child should be, as far as practicable in a given case, applied to his study of the object. First it should be described as to its qualities; next as to its uses, then as to its origin; for example, Here is an object! What color is it? What is its shape? Feel it! Taste it!, etc. If possible, have the child see the use of the object and its origin in every possible way. Just as the concrete idea of the object is imparted by verbal description and by various appeals to the senses of the child, so the different uses of the object should be brought out in describing actions that the child sees performed with it before him. This, of course, is an ideal that the teacher should try to realize as far as possible. The object would be shown to the child in different circumstances and under different aspects so as to give it always the appearance of something new and something to excite and hold the attention of the child. Take, for instance, a lesson on the word "hen." Show a paper model of the hen, the live hen in the courtyard, the color slide of the hen; the picture of the hen in the reading book; the hen alive among other domestic fowls; pictures of the hen among pictures of other birds, etc. Each new step should be taken on a different day and each time the word should be connected with the object. Write the word on the blackboard; make up the printed card for the card file and put it in its proper box. "Who wants to take the blackboard outdoors? We are going to write some words in the yard. Now in your reading books there is the figure of the hen. Next to it is the word 'hen.' Write this word in your copybooks. Who can repeat what we have said about the hen? Write down what you know about the hen." The amount of information given about a particular object will depend, of course, upon the class. The simplest description should be followed by one more minute, passing thus to speak of uses, habits, origin, etc. The writing of a simple word may be developed into a written description. But the lessons on the given object should always be short, and they should be repeated on different days. For the lessons on trees, plants, and vegetables, a garden is necessary; the children should see the seeds planted, a growing vegetable, a picture of the fruit, etc. If possible, the domestic use of the garden products should be demonstrated. This applies also to flowers. The blackboard with chalks should never be lacking in the garden. For object lessons we need toys to represent furniture, dishes, various objects used in the home, tools of different trades, rooms and the furniture that goes in each, houses, trees, a church (to build villages), etc.; dolls equipped with all the necessities for dressing. There should be a shelf for bottles containing specimens of different drinks; various kinds of cloths (for tactile exercises); the raw materials out of which they are made; demonstrations of the way they are manufactured, etc. Show also specimens of the various minerals, etc.

HISTORY

History is taught first on a little stage with living tableaux, gradually advancing to action: second, by descriptions of large illustrations and colored pictures; third, by storytelling based on slides. The teacher should strive for brevity, conciseness, and vivacity in descriptions. Historical storytelling should, as in the case of all other lessons, bring about additions of printed cards to the word boxes. Various information on the seasons, months of the year, etc., should be imparted by illustrations and pictures. Every morning the child should be asked: "What day is it? What day was yesterday? What day will tomorrow be?" and "What day of the month is it?"

GEOGRAPHY

1. Exercises on the plane for the cardinal points, with various gymnastic and guessing games. 2. Building games out-of-doors. Make a lake, an island, a peninsula, a river. 3. Carry the houses and church into the yard and construct a small village. Put the church on the north; the schoolhouse on the east; the mountain on the west; in front of the school place the national flag. 4. In the classroom fit out a room with its proper furniture to be placed on a map of the room outlined on a large chart. As the furniture is removed, make a mark on the map to indicate where each article was. Make a little village in the same way—houses, church, etc. Take away the church, etc.; mark the place of each object on the map as it is removed. Then identify each spot. "Where was the church?" "What was over here?" Thus we get a conception of the geographical map. Read the map, making use of the cardinal points. 5. Physical characteristics of regions may be shown by clay modeling to represent hills, etc. Draw outlines around each model, remove the clay and read the geographical map resulting.

MATHEMATICS

Arithmetic

The children are to count: 1 nose; 1 mouth; 1, 2 hands; 1, 2 feet; 1, 2, 3, 4 points in the insets; 1, 2, 3, 4, 5, 6 soldiers on the plane. How many blocks did they use in the building? 1, 2, 3, 4, 5, 6, 7, 8, 9. Thus for the elementary steps in counting.

Computation

Computation should be taught practically in the store from the very beginning. The shopkeeper sells one cherry for 1¢. The children have 2¢ and get two cherries. Next they get two nuts for 1¢. Place 1¢ on the counter and place two nuts beside it. Then count all the nuts and there are two for 1¢, etc. The child wants one cherry and has a nickel. The shopkeeper must give him 4¢ in change; $5 - 1 = 4$. In making change it will be observed that at first some children recognize the coins more easily by touch than by sight (motor types).

Written Numbers

Charts with the nine numbers: one for each number. Each chart has pictures representing quantities of the most varied objects arranged around the number, which is indicated by a large design on the chart. For instance: on the 1 card there is one cherry, one dog, one ball, etc. Yesterday the shopkeeper sold one cherry for 1¢. Is the cherry here? Yes, there is the cherry! And what is this? One church! And this? One cent! etc. What is this figure here? It is the number one. Now bring out the wooden figure. What is this? Number one! Put it on the figure on the chart! It is one.

Now take the charts to the store. Who has 1¢? Who has 2¢?, etc. Let us look for the number among the charts. The shopkeeper is selling three peas for 1¢. Let us look for number 3 among the charts! Numbers should be taught in the afternoon lesson in the store. The designs representing the figures should be shown the following morning. Next time the charts with the figures previously taught should be taken to the shop to be recognized again. Other numbers are brought out in the new computations. The figures for the new numbers then taught in the store should be shown the following day, etc. To make the store interesting, the topic lesson on the objects offered for sale should be frequently repeated. The child should be taught to buy only perfect objects, so that on receiving them he may examine them carefully, observing them in all their parts. He should give them back if they are not perfect or if mistakes are made by the shopkeeper in giving them out. For instance: A spoiled apple should not be accepted. "I refuse to buy it!" Beans should not be accepted for peas. Again the child refuses to buy them. He must pay only when he is sure he has been served properly (exercise in practical life).

The storekeeper will make mistakes: first, in kinds of objects, to sharpen the observation of qualities by the children who purchase; second, in the number of objects given, to accustom the child to purchasing proper quantities.

Odd and Even Numbers

Even numbers are red. Odd numbers are blue. There are: movable figures in wood; red and blue cubes in numbers corresponding to the figures on them; finally, charts with numbers drawn in color. Under each design are small red and blue squares arranged in such a way as to emphasize the divisibility of even numbers by 2 and, similarly, the indivisibility by 2 of odd numbers. In the latter case one square is always left by itself in the center.

The child places the movable numbers and the cubes on the figures on the charts. The teacher then makes two equal rows of cubes to correspond to the even numbers (red). The division is easy! But try to separate the odd numbers (blue). It is not possible! A block is always left in the middle! The child takes the figures and the blocks and arranges them on his table, imitating the design on the chart. He tries to make two equal rows of cubes for the even numbers. He succeeds. He does not succeed in doing so with the odd numbers. The numbers that can be divided thus are even; those that cannot be so divided are odd.

Number boxes: On these boxes are designed red and blue figures identical with those on the charts. The child puts into each box the number of cubes called for by the figure on the box. This exercise follows immediately the work on odd and even numbers described above. As the child transfers each series of cubes from his table to the boxes, he pronounces the number and adds odd or even.

Exercises in attention and memory: A chart of odd and even numbers in colors is placed on the teacher's desk in view of all the children. The red and blue cubes are piled on the teacher's desk. The teacher passes the wooden figures to the children and tells them to examine them. Immediately afterward the children leave their seats, go to the teacher's desk, and get the numbers that correspond to their own figures. On going back to their places they fit the cubes under the corresponding figure in the arrangement just learned. The teacher is to observe:

1. Whether the child has remembered the color of his figure (frequently a child with a red number takes the blue cubes).

2. Whether he has remembered his number.

3. Whether he remembers the proper arrangement.

4. Whether the child remembers that the chart from which he can copy is before him on the stand and whether he thinks of looking at it.

When mistakes are made, the teacher has the child correct himself by calling his attention to the chart.

Counting by Tens

(For more advanced classes)

In the store ten objects are sold for 1¢, *e.g.*, 10 beans, 1¢ for each ten.

One ten=ten, 10.

Two tens=twenty, 20.

Three tens=thirty, 30, etc.

From forty on [in English, from sixty on] the numbers are more easily learned because their names are like simple numbers with the ending "-ty" [Italian, *anta*].

Charts should be prepared (rectangular in shape) on which nine tens appear arranged one under the other; then nine cards where each ten is repeated nine times in a column; finally, numerous cards with the unit figures 1, 2, 3, 4, 5, 6, 7, 8, 9 to be fitted on the zeros on the cards where the tens are repeated nine times.

$$10 \cdot 10 \cdot 20$$
$$20 \cdot 10 \cdot 20$$
$$30 \cdot 10 \cdot 20$$
$$40 \cdot 10 \cdot 20$$
$$50 \cdot 10 \cdot 20$$
$$60 \cdot 10 \cdot 20$$
$$70 \cdot 10 \cdot 20$$
$$80 \cdot 10 \cdot 20$$
$$90 \cdot 10 \cdot 20$$

Some difficulty will be experienced with the tens where the names do not correspond to the simple numbers: 11, 12, 13, etc. The other tens, however, will be very easy. When a little child is able to count to 20, he can go on to 100 without difficulty. The next step is to superimpose the little cards on the first chart of the tens series, having the resultant numbers read aloud.

Problems

Problems are, at first, simple memory exercises for the children. In fact, the problems are solved practically in the store in the form of a game—buying, lending, sharing with their schoolmates, taking a part of what is bought and giving it to some other child, etc. The store exercises should be repeated in the form of a problem on the following morning. The children have simply to remember what happened and reproduce it in writing. Problems are next developed contemporaneously with the various arithmetical operations and computations (addition, multiplication, etc.). The teacher explains the operations starting with the problem, which becomes for the children a very amusing game. The problem, finally, becomes an imaginative exercise: "Suppose you are going to the store to buy . . ." We can ultimately arrive at real problems that require reasoning. In the store the teacher illustrates the various operations on the blackboard, using simple marks at first: "You have bought 2¢ worth of beans, at three for a cent. Let us write that down: III–III. Then let us count.

III   III

1, 2, 3, 4, 5, 6. There are six. Well, then, $3+3=6$. We can also say: two groups of III equals six; twice three, six; two times three, six; $2 \times 3 = 6$. How much is $3+3$? How much is 2×3? How much is 3×2?"

The following morning, when the written problem is given, the child should have before him for reference the computation charts with all the combinations possible.

The transition to mental computation will come after this and not before.

Sample Cards

(Addition)

$1+1=2$	$2+1=3$	$3+1=4$
$1+2=3$	$2+2=4$	$3+2=5$
$1+3=4$	$2+3=5$	$3+3=6$
$1+4=5$	$2+4=6$	$3+4=7$

(Multiplication)

$1 \times 1 = 1$	$2 \times 1 = 2$	$3 \times 1 = 3$
$1 \times 2 = 2$	$2 \times 2 = 4$	$3 \times 2 = 6$
$1 \times 3 = 3$	$2 \times 3 = 6$	$3 \times 3 = 9$

Subtraction in the same way. The development of these various operations followed logically on the practical exercise in the store, where multiplication proved to be a product of sums, division, a process of successive subtractions.

In our classes we have arithmetic lessons every day. The afternoon practice in the store prepares for the theoretical lesson of the following morning. Accordingly, on the day when the practical exercise occurs, there is no theoretical lesson and vice versa.

The decimal metric system applied to weights, measures, and coinage is taught in the same way. The store should be equipped with scales, weights, dry and liquid measures, etc. All kinds of coins should be available, including bills up to $20. Work in the store should continue to be not only a help toward arithmetical computation but also toward the preparation for practical life. For instance, when cloth is sold, some attention should be given to its actual market value; its qualities should be emphasized by feeling, etc.; and the child should be taught to observe whether the storekeeper has given him the right amount and the right quality. Making change should be mastered. The money that the children spend at the store should be earned by them as a reward for their application to study and their good behavior.

APPENDIX B

THE EDITOR

R. C. OREM, M.Ed., who received nine scholarships and grants for study at various educational institutions, has taught English and social studies from grades seven through twelve in public and private schools. For three years, he directed the training of the 900-member staff of the District of Columbia Children's Center, a complex of three institutions, each with a comprehensive education program for approximately 800 juvenile delinquents and 1,200 mentally retarded persons.

He is a former Educational Specialist with the Department of Defense and Director of Guidance Services at the Ft. Meade Army Education Center, where he had responsibility for the general educational development of military and civilian personnel. For several years he conducted programs in reading improvement and communication skills for professional adults in industry and government, including fifteen federal agencies, and for secondary students in public school systems. He serves on the Advisory Board of the Reading Reform Foundation.

While an associate with the Planning Research Corporation, he engaged in major evaluations of full-year Head Start programs for the Office of Economic Opportunity, and the first year operation of Title I of P.L. 89–10 (Elementary and Secondary Education Act) for the U.S. Office of Education. As part of the latter study, he reviewed the 586 projects selected as most innovative or exemplary of some 22,000 local projects.

He is now a consultant to Economic Systems Corporation, a division of AVCO, which is conducting an evaluation of some 100 Title I Indian projects from Alaska to Mississippi for the Bureau of Indian Affairs.

His first book, *A Montessori Handbook* (1965), has gone through several printings in clothbound (Putnam) and paperback editions (Capricorn) and, as noted in *Publisher's Weekly*, had the largest advance sale of any Capricorn book in recent years. His second Montessori book, *Montessori for the Disadvantaged* (1967, Putnam), is also available in paperback (Capricorn). *Montessori and the Special Child* is his third book in this field. Other books include *The Case for Early Reading* (1967, with George Stevens), and *Managing Student Behavior* (1968, with William Amos) both published by Warren H. Green, Inc., Publishers, St. Louis, Missouri.

He has given seminars and lectures on Montessori and early learning at the AMS training course in Greenwich, Connecticut, and New York City, and at the Montessori in-service training course for New Rochelle, New York, teachers. He is also research adviser to the Alcuin (Chicago) Montessori training program. He has spoken on a variety of Montessori-related topics in Corpus Christi, Boston, Philadelphia, Minneapolis, and other cities, and is on the editorial board of *Children's House* magazine.

THE CONTRIBUTORS

WILLIAM P. ARGY, M.D., has been Medical Director of the District of Columbia Society for Crippled Children since 1950. He is Professor of Medicine, Emeritus, of Georgetown University, and from 1931 to 1954 was Chief of Medicine, Providence Hospital, Washington, D.C., which he now serves as consultant in medicine.

He is an associate of the American Academy of Neurology, a Fellow of the American Academy for Cerebral Palsy and the American College of Physicians, and a member of the American Medical Association. He is on the board of directors of the Benedictine School for Exceptional Children, Ridgely, Maryland; the board of trustees of the Children's Rehabilitation Institute, Reisterstown, Maryland; and the advisory board of the Partridge Schools and Rehabilitation Center, Gainesville, Virginia; and the United Cerebral Palsy of Northern Virginia Development Center, Falls Church.

THOMAS J. BANTA (B.A., Psychology, Ohio State University; M.A., Experimental Psychology, and Ph.D., Social Psychology, Columbia University) is Associate Professor of Psychology in the Graduate School at the University of Cincinnati. Consulting Editor for the *Journal of Educational Research* and *Children's House*, Dr. Banta has taught at Northwestern University, the University of Wisconsin, and the University of Denver.

As Director of the Montessori Research Project, which involves eight schools in Cincinnati and schools in California, Texas, New York, Georgia, Florida, Michigan, Minnesota, and Colorado, he has directed the development of procedures for studying growth and behavior in young children, including the Cincinnati Autonomy Test Battery (CATB). His research extends as far as a school in Uganda, East Africa. He has published some thirty articles, reports, and book chapters.

LOIS-ELLIN DATTA, B.A., M.A. (Sociology), M.A. (Social Psychology), Ph.D., is a former Research Psychologist at the National Institute of Mental Health, where she conducted research on the development of exceptional individuals: the gifted, the socially deprived, and the intellectually handicapped. She is now Director of Research for Head Start. She teaches at the Catholic University of America and the University of Virginia, and has also taught at D. C. Teachers College and Bryn Mawr College. She has published widely in the fields of psychology and education.

EDITH M. DEAN, secretary to the vice-president of the California firm Northrup Ventura, has published approximately one hundred articles in *Health, Boys' Life, Family Digest,* and other magazines.

PAUL J. DUNN, M.D., a founder of the Alcuin Montessori School in Oak Park, Illinois, and the Illinois Montessori Society, has practiced pediatrics for many years, and is now Director of the Chicago Center for the Achievement of Human Potential.

He is a Fellow of the American Academy of Pediatrics and was a board member of the American Montessori Society for three years. He has also served as Assistant Clinical Professor of Pediatrics at

Stritch School of Medicine; Medical Director and co-founder of the Loretto Research Institute in Chicago ; and member of the medical advisory board of the Institutes for the Achievement of Human Potential in Philadelphia.

DAVID ELKIND, Ph.D., is Associate Professor of Psychology at the University of Rochester. He was formerly Associate Professor and Director of the Child Study Center at the University of Denver, and Assistant Professor of Medical Psychology at the U.C.L.A. School of Medicine. He has also taught at the Rhode Island College of Education Graduate School, Wheaton College, and Cambridge Junior College.

He has served as psychological consultant to the Arapahoe County, (Colorado) Court Juvenile Probation Department, the Massachusetts Pre-School Retarded Children's Program, and the Cambridge (Massachusetts) Child Guidance Clinic. He is Associate Editor of *Child Development Monographs*, Consulting Editor of *Contemporary Psychology*, and a member of the *Child Development* editorial board. He has published more than fifty articles, book chapters, and books, including (with J.H. Flavell) *Essays in Cognitive Development* (New York, Oxford), honoring Jean Piaget's seventieth birthday.

LENA L. GITTER of Washington, D.C., has studied in Austria, France, England, Holland, and the United States, and holds diplomas in early child development, Montessori kindergarten, teaching, and special education.

She conducts institutes, seminars, and study groups for parents, educators, and teacher trainees throughout the United States. She serves as consultant to public and private schools, colleges and universities.

She conducts Montessori Workshops for the Child Development Group of Mississippi (CDGM), and since 1963 has visited dozens of Montessori schools to evaluate and make recommendations. She has authored more than fifty papers, articles, and book chapters dealing with such topics as Montessori and art, special education, and the disadvantaged, including "Direction for Head Start" in

Montessori for the Disadvantaged, R.C. Orem, editor (Putnam's, 1967).

DR. HOMER HENDRICKSON, O.D., Temple City, California. After graduating from Los Angeles College of Optometry, an affiliate of the University of Southern California, Dr. Hendrickson did postgraduate study under Samuel Renshaw, Gerald N. Getman, and Newell C. Kephart.

He is presently Associate Director of the Optometric Extension Program Foundation (a nonprofit international organization dedicated to postgraduate optometric education and research), and is Western Zone Chairman and staff lecturer, Child Vision Care Section, of the foundation.

GABRIEL D. OFEISH, Ed.D. is Professor of Education and Director of the Center for Educational Technology at the Catholic University of America Graduate School of Education. He has served as Assistant Professor of Psychology at Butler University, and as Assistant Professor of Philosophy and Associate Professor of Psychology at the U.S.A.F. Academy.

Founder and first president of the National Society for Programmed Instruction, he was appointed in 1965 as the Chief Consultant on Educational Technology, Office of Economic Opportunity. A World War II combat navigator and aviation psychologist, he was awarded the Distinguished Flying Cross, the Air Medal with three Oak Leaf Clusters and numerous other medals and citations.

For his contributions to educational technology and programmed learning he has received such awards as the Air Force Association Citation of Honor, the Legion of Merit (U.S.A.F.) and the Joint Services Commendation Medal. He has published some twenty-five articles and books, including the popular *Trends in Programmed Instruction* (edited with Wesley C. Meierhenry), Washington, D.C., National Education Association.

RUTH ANN O'KEEFE, B.A., M.A., Ed.D., was a Senior Associate with the Planning Research Corporation, where she had responsibility for organizing and analyzing data obtained from approximately fifty independent research studies and reports concerned with effects of summer Head Start projects on participating children and their families. She has also participated in the evaluation of 1966 Full Year Head Start programs and 1966 Title I (Elementary and Secondary Education Act) programs for educationally disadvantaged children.

While with the Institute of Educational Research she was project director of a three-year study sponsored by the National Institute of Mental Health, to develop the Basal Progressive Choice reading program for mentally retarded children. This program was subsequently published by Science Research Associates as *Lift Off to Reading*.

She is now engaged in research studies with the Washington School of Psychiatry. She teaches "Introduction to the Education of Exceptional Children" and "Problems in Teaching Culturally Disadvantaged Children and Youth" at the Catholic University of America, and has written a number of articles on special education for professional journals. Dr. O'Keefe was awarded a four-year Seven College Conference Scholarship to Bryn Mawr College, and after graduating in 1956, was a teacher of elementary, and trainable mentally retarded, children for several years.

SYLVIA O. RICHARDSON, M.D., former editor of *Children's House*, is a distinguished pediatrician known for her outstanding work in evaluation and management of children with learning and language disabilities. She received her B.A. from Stanford University, her M.A. in Education of the Exceptional from Columbia, and her M.D. from McGill University. She is a certified Speech Pathologist, a certified Montessori teacher, and co-founder and first president of the Massachusetts Speech and Hearing Association.

Dr. Richardson has served on the faculty at Columbia, Boston, and Harvard universities, and currently is an Assistant Clinical Professor of Pediatrics at the University of Cincinnati College of Medicine. She is also Assistant Director of Learning Disabilities Program, Hamilton County Diagnostic Clinic. Formerly, she was director of the Child Study Center, University of Oklahoma Medical Center. Among her consultant appointments have been those to the National Institute of Nervous Diseases and Blindness, the Divisions of Child Health and Maternal Welfare in the states of Massachusetts and Oklahoma, and to many state and local organizations concerned with children. She is presently a consultant to the Division of Hospital and Medical Facilities and the Division of Mental Retardation of the United States Public Health Service.

She has contributed to several books and many scientific and professional journals and has lectured extensively throughout the United States. Honors include: Fellow, American Speech and Hearing Association; listing in *Who's Who of American Women* and in *Who's Who in the Southwest*; and service awards from several professional organizations. In 1964 she was named Oklahoma Woman of the Year, and in 1966 she received a citation from the Governor of Oklahoma for her services to the state in mental health planning.

GEORGE L. STEVENS, Ph.B., Loyola of Baltimore, M.A., University of Maryland, is currently working toward his doctorate in Human Development and Reading.

A former instructor of English in the University of Maryland Dean of Students Office and Director of the Reading Program of the U.S. Department of Agriculture Graduate School, he now operates his own reading consultant service in the metropolitan Washington area. He also serves as a reading specialist at Galludet College, the national college for the education of the deaf, and as instructor in education in the Graduate School of the Catholic University of America.

ROBERT WEBER, B.A., M.A., and candidate for the Ph.D. in Social Sciences, is Director of Program Development for Responsive Environments Corporation, where his responsibilities involve the development of education, training, antipoverty and other programs related to the general problem of human growth and development.

A former member of the faculty of the University of Buffalo and the University of Minnesota, he has been an editor and administrator in scientific and technical research for the Rand Corporation, the System Development Corporation, and the Lockheed Electronics Company Systems Research Center. Other positions have included

Director of the International Research Institute; Consultant to the President of Educational Testing Service; Consultant to Washington Action for Youth; and Consultant to the Office of Juvenile Delinquency (HEW) and the President's Committee on Juvenile Delinquency (Department of Justice).